Routledge Series in Information Systems

Edited by Steve Clarke (Hull University Business School, UK), M. Adam Mahmood (University of Texas at El Paso, USA), and Morten Thanning Vendelø (Copenhagen Business School, Denmark)

The overall aim of the series is to provide a range of text books for advanced undergraduate and postgraduate study and to satisfy the advanced undergraduate and postgraduate markets, with a focus on key areas of those curricula.

The key to success lies in delivering the correct balance between organizational, managerial, technological, theoretical, and practical aspects. In particular, the interaction between, and interdependence of, these often different perspectives is an important theme. All texts demonstrate a "theory into practice" perspective, whereby the relevant theory is discussed only in so far as it contributes to the applied nature of the domain. The objective here is to offer a balanced approach to theory and practice.

Information Systems is a rapidly developing and changing domain, and any book series needs to reflect current developments. It is also a global domain, and a specific aim of this series, as reflected in the international composition of the editorial team, is to reflect its global nature. The purpose is to combine state-of-the-art topics with global perspectives.

Information Systems Strategic Management: An integrated approach, 2nd edition
Steve Clarke

Managing Information and Knowledge in Organizations: A literacy approach
Alistair Mutch

Knowledge Management Primer
Rajeev K. Bali, Nilmini Wickramasinghe, Brian Lehaney

Healthcare Knowledge Management Primer
Nilmini Wickramasinghe, Rajeev K. Bali, Brian Lehaney, Jonathan L. Schaffer, M. Chris Gibbons

Systems Practice in the Information Society
José-Rodrigo Córdoba-Pachón

Business Information Systems: A primer
Brian Lehaney, Phil Lovett and Mahmood Shah

Mobile Working: Technologies and business strategies
Mahmood Hussain Shah

Mobile Working

Developments in information and communication technologies (ICTs) during the last few decades have brought about a sea change in the ways in which most people in the industrialized world work. In many organizations the ability to "work remotely" or "telecommute" has helped productivity improve. However, many of the benefits promised by the onset of "mobile working" have failed to materialize. This book explains the technology and strategic issues surrounding mobile working and presents a clear analysis of how this process can be managed.

Combining a better understanding of the state of the art in e-business technologies with a focus on how organizations can effectively provide information support for mobile working, this book will also investigate the relationship between human and organizational factors and success in mobile working.

With detailed case studies from a range of countries, this book will be useful reading on a range of courses at Masters and MBA level, including e-business, mobile technologies, operations management, technology management and change management.

Mahmood Hussain Shah leads the Security and Information Systems Research Group (SISRG) at the Lancashire Business School, University of Central Lancashire, UK. He is co-author of *Business Information Systems* (Routledge, 2011), *E-banking Management* (IGI Global, USA) and has published papers in several high-quality journals, including the *European Journal of Information Systems* and the *International Journal of Information Management*. He is leading a number of research projects in mobile security, identity theft prevention in online retailing and information security in e-banking.

Mobile Working

Technologies and business strategies

Mahmood Hussain Shah

Routledge
Taylor & Francis Group

LONDON AND NEW YORK

First published 2014
by Routledge
2 Park Square, Milton Park, Abingdon, Oxon OX14 4RN

and by Routledge
711 Third Avenue, New York, NY 10017

Routledge is an imprint of the Taylor & Francis Group, an informa business

British Library Cataloguing in Publication Data
A catalogue record for this book is available from the British Library

Library of Congress Cataloging in Publication Data
Shah, Mahmood, 1971–
    Mobile working : technologies and business strategies / Mahmood Shah.
        pages cm
Includes bibliographical references and index.
    1. Telecommuting. 2. Virtual work teams. 3. Information technology–
Management. I. Title.
    HD2336.3.S53 2013
    658.3'123–dc23
                2013015399

ISBN: 978-0-415-67823-0 (hbk)
ISBN: 978-1-315-88529-2 (ebk)

Typeset in Bembo
by Taylor & Francis Books

To my family, colleagues and friends

Contents

Case studies

Illustrations

Figures

Tables

Preface

Why read this book

Organizations are making significant investments in mobile working systems to deliver a range of types of business value, from increased efficiency and cost reduction, to improved operational effectiveness and customer service, and in some cases to innovate in ways of working to provide a competitive advantage. The age old problem of providing the right information at the right time is the main hindrance to growth in mobile working. Rapid developments in mobile technologies are improving the potential effectiveness of mobile working all the time. However, the growth of mobile working and promised benefits have fallen short of expectations so far. One of the key reasons for this, identified through my research and practice over a number of years, has been the lack of understanding and the neglect of relevant technologies, human aspects and organizational issues involved. This book will act as a guide for approaching mobile working as an organization wide project rather than just a piecemeal approach which I witness at present very often.

This book will be themed around human and organizational issues as well as the information technologies needed to support mobile working and will focus on key elements within the domain such as building a technological infrastructure, operations management, human issues and so on, reviewing their importance and the ways in which these issues can be better managed. Emphasis will be put on how issues are managed in a global, real mobile working context, thus most of the chapters will include real-world mobile working case studies carried out in several countries across the world. This book will also report the actual experiences relating to the implementation of mobile working, providing practical guidelines for practitioners and useful cases for education and training purposes.

The domain of mobile technologies is covered by a wide range of texts but none of these are specifically related to their use in supporting mobile working. This book will therefore complement other books in the area of mobile communications such as Kenneth C. Laudon (2006, 2nd edition) *Mobile Communications*, Chaffey D. (2009) *e-business and E-commerce*.

Objectives of this book

- Provide a better understanding of state-of-the-art mobile technologies with a (unique to this text) focus on how they can effectively provide information support for mobile working.
- Integrate the relationship between human and organizational factors and success in mobile working.
- Explore the theoretical, conceptual and practical issues in managing modern mobile technologies to effectively support mobile working.
- Provide detailed case studies, both in the UK and internationally with a focus on providing practical guidelines for dealing with critical organization issues in developing and supporting mobile working.

Coverage

The book will begin with an introduction to generic technical, human and organizational issues in mobile working to form a rationale for the text. A background chapter will review mobile working as it stands at present, typical services on offer, typical uses and the supplier, information management and user issues which emanate from this.

Cases in managing information for mobile working will be provided at the start of chapters and where necessary in other places throughout the text, covering all aspects of each case in a standard format (based on the model used within ACIT). This will be the primary vehicle for providing practitioner focus and will be referred to extensively within the text as a link between the practice, theory and conceptual issues.

The focus will be on technical (mobile technologies as well as those which compliment mobile working), human, operational, managerial and strategic organizational issues in mobile working. Other issues, such as regulatory, legal or environmental requirements will also be included. New theoretical constructs underpinning research and practice in mobile working will be explained and related to the practical issues such as business continuity, security and policies for productive use within the domain.

Who should use this book

The main readership is expected to be split into three areas:

- Final year undergraduate students and masters level students in the UK and internationally, on courses primarily in information systems, mobile technologies, operations management, technology management and change management.
- As a supporting text for postgraduate level business or Information Systems students.

- It could also be used as a practical guide for mobile working practitioners in the UK and other countries who wish to understand more about the mobile-working-related issues.

It is accepted that serving such a wide audience is not an easy task, and that, in particular, meeting the needs of both a practitioner and academic audience is problematic. With this in mind, it will be a specific objective within the text to blend these issues, bringing the theoretical constructs to life through applied examples.

Structure of the book

The book is split into nine chapters.

Chapter one develops a rationale for the text and introduces definitions of the generic technical, human and organizational issues in mobile working. Chapter two includes: the needs and drivers for mobile working; historical development mobile working; the need for information systems technologies to support mobile working; social and business drivers of mobile working as well as the key developments in technologies and business practices which make mobile working a viable option for a far greater number of organizations. This chapter will also briefly cover the most common types of mobile working applications.

Chapter three covers managerial issues in mobile working and operational issues in mobile working. The main focus is on how mobile working operations run and what managerial issues arise as a result. Some suggestions for dealing with these issues will also be included.

Chapter four addresses the evolution of mobile technologies and their typical uses, providing background information for the rest of the text. It describes the common mobile technologies, systems architectures and middleware options. It also covers the possible future directions and implications for mobile technologies. Other topics include mobile devices, interface issues and the technical infrastructure required to support the smooth functioning of mobile working.

Due to the newness of mobile working, there are still a number of usability and trust issues which need to be addressed to achieve widespread adoption by employees. Chapter five analyses these issues and offers practical advice on how to deal with the resistance to use such technology and the lack of trust.

There are many security problems associated with mobile technologies, owing particularly to the open nature of these systems. Security is a key legal requirement and businesses must do their utmost to protect their own as well as their customer's valuable information. Chapter six covers these as well as the need to plan for other critical events and other system failures. This chapter provides guidelines on how to manage security issues as well as possibilities of system failures.

Systematic project management is an important concept in the implementation of new technologies. Chapter seven discusses reasons for treating technology implementation as an organization-wide project. It also covers the most common methods of project management and technological tools such as PRINCE2 which help manage projects.

Mobile working often results in significant changes in the way an organization functions, thus having the need for managing change. Chapter eight covers key issues in change management and common approaches/methods to managing mobile-working-related organizational change. Chapter nine is a review and summary of the content of the book and discusses theoretical and practical implications of the ideas covered.

Pedagogical/interactive features of the book

1. Each chapter begins with a case study. Chapters are summarized and questions for review and discussion will be given at the end of each chapter.
2. References and suggested further reading are given at the end of each chapter.
3. Case studies and key issues covered by the cases are included where appropriate.
4. A Glossary is provided as an appendix to explain the jargon and technical terms commonly used in the domain and in this book.

Acknowledgements

My gratitude is owed to colleagues of the past and present for their help and support in producing this book including Professor Steve Clarke, Professor Ray Paul, Professor John Ward, Zhi Qi Lin, Joseph Black, Abdullah Matilo and Farjad Shah. I also thank Routledge T&F Group for the support they provided during the development of this book and also for the valuable comments from reviewers which helped improve this book. Furthermore, my thanks will have to go to my family for their patience and support during the writing of this book.

1

INTRODUCTION TO THE BOOK AND MOBILE WORKING

The past decade has seen dramatic advances in mobile technologies in terms of functionality, power, usability, connectivity and affordability. Therefore they have become widespread among individuals in the most advanced countries. These smart mobile devices can also be used by a variety of organizations to run their operations, a phenomenon often referred to as mobile working. Organizations generally make investments in mobile working systems to deliver business value. The nature of this value can range from efficiency and cost reduction, to operational effectiveness, to possibly providing a source of competitive advantage.

Several factors, described by Schrott and Gluckler (2004), have contributed to the decision to invest in mobile technologies. First, immense efforts have been undertaken towards restructuring in order to reduce the level of hierarchy within organizations and to create more permeable internal and external boundaries. Employees do not have to be co-located with their colleagues to interact. Instead, the vision of future work scenarios constitutes settings in which globally distributed individuals may work together simultaneously without sharing physical co-presence. The second factor that has contributed to this development has been the availability of technological infrastructure. Third, the number of providers for mobile devices has been increasing steadily. The variety of personal digital assistants, notebooks, tablets with mobile access and smart phones has never been greater. Finally, the shrinking costs of data transmission and the sponsoring of devices have additionally catalysed the distribution of mobile technologies and amplified the growth of the worldwide mobile market. Together with a strong emphasis on collaboration and group work, these factors have led to the establishment of mobile working as an integral part of many people's daily working life.

Despite the above mentioned popularity of mobile devices, the expected rise in mobile working has not materialized yet, but the arrival of new smart phones and tablets, along with other developments mentioned in this chapter, could possibly produce the right conditions for the long-predicted 'take-off'. First, there is the phenomenal rise in prominence of a new generation of digitally literate consumers who have acquired familiarity with new technologies through the constant use of online culture (such as social networking sites) and the need for mobile phones as an essential product for their everyday lives. Second, the availability of technically safer and speedier internet connections could bring about greater trust in the use of mobile technologies by people as well as providing greater security against fraud. Third, major investment in the infrastructure of mobile communications has resulted in big players seeing mobile working as a source of return and investment along with individual consumers, so they actively develop mobile working solutions and promote them aggressively.

Advancements in mobile internet-technology are of pivotal importance when discussing how fast mobile working might achieve the levels of future growth ascribed to it by optimistic trend forecasters. The introduction of third, and subsequently fourth, generation 'smart phones' that will allow subscribers convenience and ease of access to surf the world wide web at ever-increasing speeds appears to provide the security and assurance needed by businesses in general to enable mobile working to leap forward in line with confident predictions in the sector.

Workers' complaints, up to now, have centred on technical deficiencies, especially the combination of sluggish internet connections, which take a long time to load web pages, and the fact that, once loaded, the connections are often quickly lost. Reports of difficulties in typing information on a small, mobile device's keypad or errors in input on touch screen keypads are also common. However, with the introduction of smart phones and tablets onto the market by marquee brands such as Apple, HTC, Samsung and Nokia, those problems of weak connection and awkward-to-use keys appear to have been resolved by virtue of the increased capacity of 4G connections, with higher data speeds and easy-to-use touch-screen keyboards. These innovations afford the potential to change the way people use mobile devices, and therefore make it possible to bridge the gap between the expectations and actual experience of businesses with regards to mobile working.

One of the challenges faced in reading the literature is discerning whether or not scholars are writing about, or indeed considering, the same or similar questions or concepts. The literature can be very confusing in this respect. Often, similar terms are used in different ways and have different meanings attached to them. In this section, key terms and concepts encountered in the literature are compared, contrasted and defined. The objective of this initial analysis is to provide a platform for a uniform assessment and understanding of what it is that is being considered in the literature.

It's important that we define mobile working at the beginning of this book. **Mobile working** for example is different from simply remote working or home working. For the purpose of our research, mobile working means 'enabling workers to work away from home or the office by providing them with suitable mobile input/output devices and relevant resources and managerial support'.

Mobile working may be confused with Mobile Commerce or M-commerce. For the purpose of this book, we will use the Oxford Dictionary definition which defines it as 'commercial transactions conducted electronically by mobile phone' (www. oxforddictionaries.com) and may be understood, therefore, to include the commercial use of any hand-held device with the capacity to utilize a portable internet connection, such as PDAs, mobile phones, tablets and laptop computers via a dongle.

The above explanation may imply that any use of mobile devices for work purposes is mobile working, but for the purpose of this book, we will portray mobile working as a much more comprehensive business solution. It often requires good computing infrastructure within a company as well as a comprehensive re-organization of a company in terms of human resources and the way its operations work. This book is providing an overview of these technological and business issues.

2

AN OVERVIEW

Mobile working

Case study: Automobile Association (AA)

This case study was prepared by the author to facilitate class discussion rather than illustrate effective or ineffective management practices. Only publicly available material has been used to write this case and it does not reflect any opinions of employees or management at this organization.

For the Automobile Association (AA), a motor breakdown service, mobile technology has brought real-time communication to a workforce that has always been predominantly field-based (Antony 2004). On the road, the organization has over 3,500 patrol staff, managers and engineers using laptops for computerized vehicle diagnosis and communication with control centres. It also has 180 employed staff working from home, taking emergency calls routed to them as if they were in a call centre, plus traditional office-based staff working flexibly.

From a human resource point of view, the AA sees regular meetings between mobile staff and managers and sets clear performance objectives as a key to managing staff. They also see a change of management approach as essential to making mobile working a success. Sarah Stacey, HR business manager for the AA, says

> There has to be face-to-face interaction because it's easy for individuals to become isolated. Crucially, it needs a change in attitude. Management has to relax and move from a mindset of physical presence to one of outcomes and clearly defined measures and objectives.

AA patrol staff and engineers have always worked in the field so suitability for working alone is a selection criterion of the role. But transforming office based staff into 'virtual call centre' workers meant HR needed to ensure they were suited to working at home.

They had a mixed experience in this regard. It worked well in many cases and productivity was higher. In other cases, individuals have come back into the office. For some people, the social interaction of working is very important to be able to perform well. Although there have been challenges managing mobile workers for the AA, it has paid off. They claim that mobile working gives them tremendous flexibility. They can turn the tap on and off quite accurately to match times when most people are driving, such as to and from work. The AA case is a human resources view and demonstrates that despite some problems, mobile working could bring many benefits to some organizations.

Introduction

This chapter will explain the concept of mobile working and discuss both the social and business drivers of mobile working as well as the key developments in technologies and business practices which make mobile working a viable option for an increasing number of organizations. Although it seems that mobile working is growing, some argue that mobile working will take a long time to be widely adopted. This is largely due to the limitations in current mobile technologies, the inability of current business structures to effectively implement and support mobile working and doubts about their benefits such as efficiency or productivity. This chapter will discuss some of these issues in detail.

Types of Mobile Working

A detailed discussion about mobile working would be incomplete without the mention of the types of mobility. We need to understand this issue from three points of views (Kakihara and Sorensen 2004), including: spatial mobility, temporal mobility and contextual mobility.

Spatial mobility

Spatial mobility is the most immediate aspect of mobility in our social lives (tourism and business travel). It may also include the mobility of objects which could follow a much more complex and diverse route than people (for example, the Sony Walkman). It may also include the mobility of symbols (for example, global satellite television networks and the Internet). It implies that physical distance is no longer a fundamental aspect of the interaction and a team or an organization can effectively work together without being in the same physical location.

Temporal mobility

By using asynchronous ICT applications (for example, email) people are able to deal with multiple tasks simultaneously. It is no longer strictly necessary to share the same time for effective interaction.

Such "instantaneity" of time in the contemporary society in general and in cyberspace in particular further increases the poly-chronicity of human activities.

Contextual mobility

Contextual mobility is about the influence of people's cultural background, particular situation or mood and mutual recognition etc., on work. Due to the advancements in mobile technology, people nowadays can easily interact with others while being relatively free from such contextual constraints, interacting with people in largely different contexts. In this sense, the relationship between interaction among people and contexts in which they are is becoming mobilized in terms of flexible patterns of interaction across different contexts.

As in Figure 2.1, all three types of mobility overlap each other. Hence, when considering mobility, or more specifically the interaction between mobile workers, we need to understand it from all three types of mobility.

The type of mobility relevant to a work context depends on whether access provided to the workers is real time online access or offline asynchronous access. Real-time accessibility requires much more robust and secure back-end systems and relatively more sophisticated mobile equipment. Asynchronous access is much cheaper and suitable for situations where a two-way real time interaction is not required, such as meter reading.

Types of mobile workers

Mobile workers are a diversified group of people. They range from healthcare providers to insurance claims adjusters to blue collar service workers. For the most part,

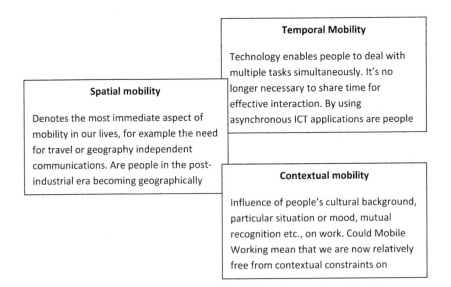

FIGURE 2.1 Three types of mobility and overlap

they are accessing unique applications that specifically support their work function. Some examples of these applications include knowledge sharing, data collection, equipment maintenance, inspection and work order access. Therefore, each worker group may have its own unique considerations depending on the environment they work in and the task at hand (York and Pendharkar 2004). A survey taken by the Yankee Group Anywhere Enterprise in 2008 which was named "Large: 2008 U.S. Fixed-Mobile Convergence/IP Communications Survey" indicates mobile workers are becoming increasingly more diverse range of occupations as illustrated in Figure 2.1. There are many ways to classify these mobile workers, and one of the easiest ways to categorize these workers is to divide them by work surroundings and work habits, for example, IDC (2011a) classifies the work groups as: office-based mobile workers, non-office-based mobile workers and home-based mobile workers.

Office-based mobile workers

The main characteristic of office-based mobile workers is their primary workplace is the office (IDC, 2011a). And it can be divided into two categories based on work habits: mobile professionals and occasionally mobile workers. *Mobile professionals* are considered as any employee who is out of the office more than 20 percent of the work time. This kind of job function requires the employee to not be tied to a single physical location who need to travel, such as salespeople, business consultants, etc. Moreover, the travelling is generally between the office and visitors. *Occasionally mobile workers* are those whose primary work is in the office but will be away from their physical location less than 20 per cent of their work time.

Non-office-based mobile workers

Non-office-based mobile workers use mobile equipment to carry out their work but without a traditional work environment, and it includes mobile field workers and mobile on-location workers (IDC, 2011a). *Mobile Field workers* are also known as mobile data collectors and their main purpose is to perform tasks on customer sites. So these workers move from location to location such as package deliverers, technicians, etc. *Mobile on-location workers* are those who work at a specific location but outside of an office environment, and they may work indoors (e.g. restaurant, warehouse), outdoors (e.g. construction site), or in mixed environment (IDC, 2011a). The main difference between mobile on-location workers and mobile field workers is the former typically work within a specific area, as the specific location is the primary workplace.

Home-Based Mobile Workers

Home-based mobile workers are those who use their home as the primary workplace all or part of the time, and this category includes telecommuters and mobile home-based business workers (IDC, 2011a). *Telecommuters* consist of corporate employees who work from home during normal working hours. *Mobile home-based business workers* are those business owners who manage the business from home.

Temporary mobile workers

There are also some mobile workers who do not fit into the categories concluded above, such as travellers, who are mobile office professionals or repair or service workers, or home-based mobile workers, who work when they are in transit. Visitors are those who are visiting another physical location; after-hour workers made up of office-based workers who continue work at home after normal business hours.

Types of use

Mobile technology has experienced enormous developments in recent years. To assess the potential productivity gains, cost savings and competitive advantages that can result from the use of mobile technology, the use of mobile technology has become increasingly important to businesses and industries (Allan and Andre, 2006). As a result, more and more people (as illustrated in Figure 2.2 are working as mobile workers to deal with different types of use, and the mobile usage needs can vary greatly across industry, business type and mobile worker type (IDC, 2011a)). So in order to optimize the mobile services, it is important for mobile vendors to identify the different types of use for mobile technology based on diversified customer needs across the industries.

There are several types of uses of mobile technologies. Some of the most common include:

1. **Information access and exchange**: This is the simplest and the most common type of use by mobile workers. The type of systems and mobile devices required for this may vary depending on the nature of the work. In some occasions, mobile workers need to access the office files and documents from different places, no matter where they are and when there is a necessity (e.g. train, conference, coffee room or with a customer). With immediate access to the needed information, it can improve the employee's productivity, synchronise all the company's resources and enhance customer care.
2. **Use of corporate applications/transactions**: This often requires relatively sophisticated back end systems and mobile devices because real-time access to corporate applications needs reasonable computing power as well as good visual display equipment.
3. **Collaborative and team activities**: These environments require participants to interact with the shared data, so adaptation of the media for certain participants may hinder other participants' comprehension and the efficiency of the communication (Branco 2001). The effectiveness of the interaction between the participants can result in the efficient execution of business processes to achieve long-term success.
4. **Financial transactions:** Mobile technology provides mobile workers with access to the financial services of different banks. They can make payments

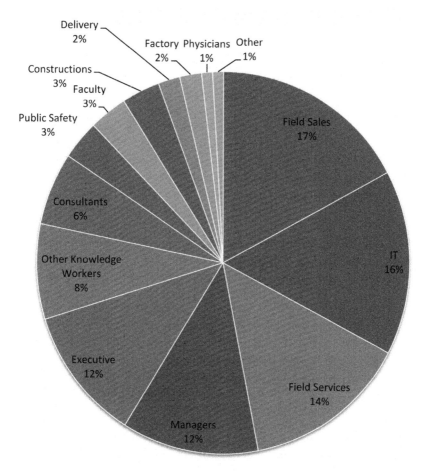

FIGURE 2.2 Mobile worker diversity
(adapted from: IDC, 2011a)

promptly instead of trying to utilise time-consuming traditional transfer services. Therefore, the business processing time can be reduced significantly and improve productivity.

5. **Use of tracking systems:** Mobile workers can use tracking systems such as Global Positioning System (GPS) to locate the precise position of the user, customer or other asset. The Global Positioning System is a satellite-based navigation system made up of a network of 24 satellites placed in earth's orbit and it can be accessed almost anywhere in the world at anytime and in any weather condition (Allan and Andre, 2006). There are two main uses of this technology: person tracking and product tracking. First, it can be used by mobile workers (e.g. sales people, technicians who work at customers' sites) to seek their customers efficiently. Secondly, the tracking system can help mobile workers to track products through the supply chain from grower to retailer (Vodafone, 2011). Therefore,

mobile workers can track the items effectively and improve supply chain efficiency. For example, according to a report by Vodafone (2011) regarding mobile and agriculture value chain, mobile phone technology has been applied extensively by African farmers to increase agricultural income and productivity. Most of the African farmers need to deal with large networks of small-scale farms, retailers, aggregators, distributors and exporters. With the help of a tracking system, the farmers can locate their suppliers and customers effectively for product delivery. Also, mobiles are used to log the location, quality and quantity of food items at key points in the supply chain, and the mobile workers (e.g. from distribution centres) can use mobile camera phones to scan product barcodes, providing details of the items and then sending the information to a central system, and the information can be used by different people (e.g. retailers, exporters and distributors) for a detailed view of product movements (Vodafone, 2011).

6. **Administrative support:** Administrative support applications such as calendars, contacts, reminders, notes, etc. provide an essential effort to the organization of work, which increases the efficiency of data management and results in greater productivity.

To realize these types of uses, there are some issues in techniques that need to be overcome. First of all, in order to achieve the real time information, how do we ensure the required data can be efficiently uploaded and downloaded from the system? Second, in order to be convenient for technicians, the mobile device should be compact: how do we ensure the small devices are capable in dealing with the tasks smoothly (e.g. sufficient storage space, working duration, processing power, graphics requirement, etc.)? Third, multiple participants may access and modify the same file at the same time so how do we avoid the collision? Finally, if corporate applications are installed in mobile devices, how do we integrate the different mobile phone systems with the applications?

Benefits of mobile working

Many organizations are attracted by the claimed productivity benefits of mobile working, lowering the demand for office space and reducing travel time (or turning it into productive time). Many employees are also attracted to mobile working since they see it as offering greater flexibility and perhaps giving them greater control over their work life balance. This section is a discussion of these issues.

Improved performance

Mobile working means that staff working at client sites can be in constant contact with their organization and other mobile colleagues. The result of this is that one may get instant responses to queries and they can have access to the most up-to-date information. Now, instead of having to type up notes or update the database on their return to the office, staff can enter information directly onto the system. Likewise, with the additional information available to them, they can offer a more complete service to clients. For example, instead of simply demonstrating a product with a laptop, they could connect to a company system; give clients the latest prices and stock figures; and even place an order on the spot. This can mean more sales and better customer service (DTI 2005). These functionalities, if utilized properly, can result in enhanced employee and organizational performance.

Case study: South West London Community NHS Trust (adapted from Microsoft, 2006)

This case study was prepared by the author to facilitate class discussion rather than illustrate effective or ineffective management practices. Only publicly available material has been used to write this case and it does not reflect any opinions of employees or management at this organization.

A primary care organization, South West London Community NHS Trust wanted to give healthcare workers access to patient information and the ability to update records while in the field, thus improving health services across a range of departments. Caroline Stones, Project Manager for South West London Community NHS Trust, explains, "We needed to collect data for statistical analysis, but we also needed to establish a system that would help staff to manage their caseloads, administer treatments, and look up patient histories."

Ian Cowles, Director of Corporate Development and Consumer Affairs for South West London Community NHS Trust, says "One example of how we could benefit from this would be if there was an outbreak of a disease like TB. This shows how important it is to get vital information to the relevant healthcare workers instantly. With a mobile Pocket PC solution, we can react instantly to that kind of situation."

The organization identified the need for peripatetic staff to access clinical information and caseloads from remote locations and to use this information in the management of their clients. The NHS Trust selected Comwise, an integrated community information system from healthcare solution provider in4tek. Comwise is used by district nurses, health visitors, therapists and other medical staff to collect, update and access information. A mobile version of the system, called Venice, was deployed on Pocket PCs.

It was supposedly easy to get staff to use the mobile devices. "Clinicians were generally very quick to learn how to use Pocket PCs because many were familiar with Windows," Cowles says. "This means that we have reduced training costs compared to those normally associated with IT implementation. Even the people who had never even used a PC before were quick to learn how to use the device.

"We are able to distribute information easily and quickly to people who are in the field," Cowles continues. "The data collection side of the solution also has many advantages. It provides extra clinical information and integrates well

> with the existing infrastructure. This means that it is easier to plan and develop better services for the future."

Mobile computing does provide an opportunity to improve safety and increase efficiency and productivity for nurses at the point of care (HealthDataManagement 2005). Mobile computing can also lead to a competitive advantage in some industries (Varshney 2000). In addition, it can help improve workflow and efficiency as well as reduce costs and risk management (Porn and Patrick 2002).

Productivity

With mobile working, time spent travelling between locations can be used productively using mobile technologies described in this document. A simple calculation of the benefits this offers can be quite surprising. If employees spend a total of only ten hours a week travelling, that's over 500 hours a year, potentially tens of thousands of pounds of lost productivity a year (DTI 2005). Some of this lost productivity could be recovered if mobile working was implemented.

Case study: British Gas (Source: Leadent Solutions, 2012)

This case study was adapted by the author to facilitate class discussion rather than illustrate effective or ineffective management practices. Only publicly available material has been used to write this case and it does not reflect any opinions of employees or management at this organization.

British Gas is the largest central heating and gas appliance installation company in the UK, installing over 110,000 central heating systems each year. From their customer contact centre in Stockport, a team of 100 plan, schedule and dispatch customer work appointments to field service engineers across the length and breadth of the UK.

British Gas recognized that their ability to achieve a step-change in operational efficiency had been held back by a heavily regimented work scheduling process and reliance on paper-based work orders. Within its planning team, inflexible systems and work prioritisation processes had stifled its ability to optimize work schedules and efficiently utilize its field engineers. Operationally, receipt of work orders and job completion data on paper had caused a reliance on field managers to coordinate the work of field engineers and to ensure that customer satisfaction was achieved. This had led to a reactive management style, 'fire-fighting' behaviours and negative customer feedback.

According to the solution provider Leadent Solutions: Applying our innovative 'Transformation Approach' we developed an in-depth understanding of opportunities for improvement within existing processes, systems, cultural behaviours and customer feedback. Working in partnership with employees at all levels, we developed and delivered a pilot to test the use of 'smart planning' processes. This incorporated the use of hand-held devices for field engineers to receive and accept work along with a wide range of process simplification measures, designed to focus maximum attention on the delivery of customer satisfaction.

Through open-working, adopting new practices and trialling mobile technology we were able to:

- Demonstrate the value of optimizing the work schedule process through application of 'smart planning' techniques.
- Strengthen the working relationships between field-based and back-office support teams.
- Undertake first-time systemization of the field-based employees through tailored training and open communication.
- Test the value of issuing electronic work orders, attaining visibility of work-in-progress and effectively capturing job completion data.
- Utilize status updates and job completion data to improve performance management capabilities.

This resulted in:

- A sustained improvement in operational performance and customer experience.
- A marked increase in resource utilization and field engineer productivity through effective planning.
- Real desire by everyone involved to be successful and to help improve customer efficiency.

One example of increased productivity resulting from mobile working is access to design and mapping data; for instance, an architect who confers with construction administrators at job sites, a repair technician who fixes multi-million dollar industrial machines on the shop floor, a utility company field worker who repairs downed lines, a facilities manager who tracks the assets of a building complex or a telecommunications field crew that need to ensure correct line connections. Each one of them can benefit from this constant access. All these professionals take large paper drawings to the field. The prints are usually costly, cumbersome to carry and often out-of-date. Quite regularly, these professionals get to the job site and then realise that they do not have all the required drawings. They are forced to drive back to the office or work on-site without all the information on hand. When working on paper drawings or maps, corrections are traditionally made by hand directly on the paper; these notes not only spoil the drawing but also make it difficult to read. Back at the office, the revisions will have to be interpreted manually, along with the digital drawings which is very time consuming. These people could benefit from remote access to digital drawings and maps and the potential savings are great (Revathy 2004).

With increased productivity, there could be a loss of jobs. Some companies are reluctant to suggest that there has been any effect on field force numbers from these changed working practices, but clearly massive productivity increases don't equate to a need for extra staff (Stedman 2004). The biggest impact is felt in the depots, rather than in the field. British Gas went from having 17,000 support staff to just 4,000. This is bad news for staff, but good news for companies, which means that this route is likely to be one that more and more utilities follow (Stedman 2004).

Further, Perry et al. (2001) discussed 'dead time' (e.g. railway stations, hotel rooms, etc.) which is indicative of the current rudimentary state of the discussion. It is also indicative of the potential for future usage where higher bandwidth can expand utilisation. The crucial point is Perry's criticism that even with mobile technology, the best that can be achieved is 'zombie time' (i.e., time that is partially resuscitated) because it can only be used inefficiently and cannot be utilised for sequential work activities that are the norm in work environments.

With a new generation of smaller, cheaper mobile devices, organizations can match technology to most of the employees' needs. For example, while sales staff might still need laptops, warehouse workers might have portable barcode scanners attached to back-end systems to check stocks and senior staff PDAs, smart phones or tablets to keep track of business operations, monitor staff activities and check their emails and appointments (DTI 2005). Figures published in the *Personnel Today* magazine in February show that many HR managers think mobile working provides greater workforce motivation and increased productivity (Antony 2004).

Barriers

There are many factors limiting the broad appeal of wireless computing. The biggest barriers are ergonomics and usability as well as the lack of practical, personal and timely interaction tools (Barbash 2001). Subsequently, workflows for mobile workers today are largely paper-based and lack automation and back end integration (Spriestersbach 2001). This section briefly discusses these issues.

User acceptance

The world of work is dominated by the geographically fixed office with its secure accountability and surveillance opportunities for managers. Being a mobile worker imposes considerable discipline issues on individuals. Embracing wireless technology requires some significant but realisable changes in working methods and work organization which could lead to many users not adopting mobile working, resulting in failure of mobile working projects (Grantham and Tsekouras 2004).

Apart from changes in working pattern, user trustworthiness is another main concern. A research conducted by Truste and Harris Interactive (2011) reveal the concerns when users try to apply mobile applications on smartphones. Consumer hesitancy acts as a blockage to the usage of applications on smartphones. The study, summarized in Figure 2.3, suggests that privacy is the biggest concern when using a mobile device: consumers expect more transparency and control over what personal information is collected and how it is shared (Truste, 2011). Thirty-eight per cent of the investigated suggest privacy is the most important concern when applying mobile applications, followed by security (26 per cent); identity tracking (19%); and the sharing of information with or without permission (14 per cent).

Suitability and performance of mobile technologies

Mobile technologies are still dogged by limitations such as limited battery life, unreliable network connections, volatile access points, risk of data loss, portability, processing power, display capabilities of most mobile devices and concerns about location discovery. These limitations are still one of the biggest barriers in the adoption of mobile working.

Complexity

There are a bewildering number of options when it comes to mobile computing. For example, applications generally available on desktops and normally not provided on mobile devices, so mobile users don't have access to the data. Also, it is possible to

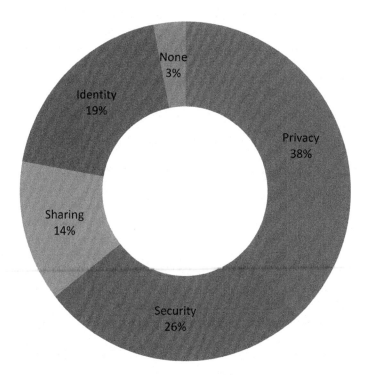

FIGURE 2.3 Primary concern when using mobile apps
(Adapted from: Truste, 2011)

spend anything from a few hundred to millions of pounds on any combination of mobile hardware, software and networks without realizing any real benefits.

High costs

With falling prices of mobile devices, one may perceive that mobile working is cheap to implement. However, it is important to remember that technology costs are only a small proportion of the likely total costs. This implies that the real cost of mobile working could be much greater than promised savings (York and Pendharkar 2004).

Perceived loss of managerial control

Managers are often hostile to mobile working because they may perceive it as a possible cause of loss of control over what is going on within an organization. A survey carried out by the *Wireless Networks* magazine found that one-fifth of managers think managing these employees is just too difficult (Antony, 2004). This could be due to the lack of understanding about mobile working and could be helped with training.

Adverse effects on work-life balance

The introduction of new technology can create new challenges as information consumers must change the way they work and potentially break bad information seeking habits (Evans, 2004). The boundary between work and personal life slowly disappears as people use mobile communication technology during weekends and holidays for business purposes as well as for personal purposes while being at work. Once familiar with the new potential of being always connected, people also experience the disadvantages of being always accessible (Kellaway, 2011) and adjust their initial manner of use (Peters and Allouch, 2005).

Inefficiency

The proliferation of personal information devices such as home computers, mobile phones and digital organizers coupled with the rise of new media such as email and the World Wide Web have forever altered the way in which information consumers work and play. These fragmented information channels often result in inefficient working patterns as users switch from device to device and between different media (Evans, 2004).

Another concern that is critical for mobile workers is knowledge management. Since field workers are usually alone most of the day in remote locations, they have issues with staying abreast of ongoing development in other projects as well as their enterprise in general (York and Pendharkar, 2004). This may have profound implications for their career development, morale and productivity, resulting in inefficient working patterns.

High roaming cost

Due to the development of the global economy, employees need to do the business from different networks, countries or territories where the home service provider has no network service license which will largely increase mobile expenses. This is a major source of revenue for mobile operators and has been assumed as a potentially anti-competitive industry practice for inter-member country roaming (Nortel, 2008). For example, according to Nortel, American subscribers roaming in Germany might pay up to $1.99 per minute and executives travelling to China have been known to rack up roaming charges in excess of $1,000 per trip.

Lack of access to critical data

Another barrier which limits the broad appeal of mobile computing is mobile workers who are being denied access to the business data. According to Gareth (2011), a research based on interviews with IT decision makers at 700 firms world-wide has been taken by a business intelligence vendor: Information Builders. The result shows the access to business applications (e.g. enterprise resource planning system, customer relationship management system) through mobile devices is restricted to about a third of staff. About three-quarters of middle managers have timely access to data, but just two thirds of the senior executive team enjoy the access and less than half of operational staff, or support staff, have such access. Furthermore, three quarters of firms agree that making operational data more available can result in better decision making or improved business relationships (Gareth, 2011).

Security issues

For most industries, the biggest barrier to going mobile is being concerned about security, as mobility is still a new concept for businesses and there is no standard security agreement for the use (Kate, 2011). Data security issues mainly relate to secure mobile networks and secure access to corporate applications. Armstrong (2010) suggests the biggest issue with mobile adoption is getting people comfortable with the security on their phone, as people don't understand the data in the airwaves as secure and they seem to be more comfortable with their personal computers. Moreover, there may be uncertainty about who should take the responsibility when there is a data breach, such as the mobile user, the mobile carrier or the network providers. So being able to set and maintain industry-wide standards about how to manage data is important, and it would be a long way in helping to adopt mobile working. Due to the importance of this topic, approximately half a chapter is devoted to it later in this book.

Interruptions and network coverage gaps

Mobile users expect to enhance the ability to be productive when out of the office and connectivity which refers to mobile network coverage will be one of the main issues. The dead spots (e.g. rural areas, parking garages, elevators, inside large manu-facturing area, etc.) interrupt service and connectivity and cause performance issues for the device and applications (Sandra and Nathan, 2008).

Poor user interface

For the most part, UI is not intuitive as a mobile was not designed to use multiple modes of communication, which makes it difficult for mobile workers to effectively and efficiently use the forms of communications that are available to them (Zeus, 2008).

Difficult device chosen

Many enterprises are still not distributing devices to the work force, as they find it difficult to decide which devices to use when making the shift to a mobile environment (Kate, 2011). According to one piece of research, more than 60 per cent mobile workers prefer to have their own equipment rather than carrying something provided by an employer (Kate, 2011). At present most mobile workers carry multiple devices such as an iPhone for personal use and a Blackberry which has been embedded with corporate applications for work.

Difficult content chosen

The question of which content and business information should be accessible through mobile channels is another barrier which many companies are still trying to figure out (Kate, 2011). And in some cases, mobile workers can get the content via email, which can also be accessed on the mobile application.

Chapter summary

In this chapter we discussed different types of mobility such as spatial mobility, temporal mobility and contextual mobility. We also looked at different types of mobile workers who range from healthcare providers to insurance claims adjusters to blue collar service workers and each group has a different set of requirements as well as different types of problems.

Finally, we discussed benefits and drawbacks of mobile working. Most of the drawbacks actually mirror benefits. For example, a commonly cited benefit of mobile working is 'work-life' balance but in some contexts it is also cited as a drawback. The same is true for 'productivity' where in some situations mobile working is perceived as a great success whereas in others, it is perceived as a cause of productivity loss. This implies that benefits may be realised when an organization establishes a clear need for mobile working and plans and implements it in a holistic manner taking most technological, organizational and social factors into account. In the absence of a realistic and systematic approach, an organization may experience some of the drawbacks discussed above.

3

KEY ISSUES IN MOBILE WORKING

Case study: Avaya

This case study was prepared by the author to facilitate class discussion rather than illustrate effective or ineffective management practices. Only publicly available material has been used to write this case and it does not reflect any opinions of employees or management at this organization.

Communications company Avaya has about 60 per cent of staff working mobile during a typical month (Antony, 2004). The HR director for Avaya, UK, Ireland and the Nordics, says, "We get more effort and energy from staff. There's no journey to and from work and if there's something pressing to organize at home, it can be fitted in around work. It reduces stress and can cut costs".

Avaya has sales and service staff in the field communicating by mobile phone, laptop and desktop PC. Office-based staff, such as finance and HR, are given the option to work from home when it suits the business. Avaya's HR team has learnt that managing mobile working staff brings new demands. They claim that mobile working needs a management style based on outcomes and objectives. Instead of being used to seeing people all the time, one has to measure performance against clear outcomes. Managers have to ensure the same feedback is given to mobile staff as they would get in the office and there is joint accountability for achieving goals. At the end of the day, staff are still going to have an appraisal so working at home is not a soft option.

For Avaya, mobile working is now a business imperative and shows what can be achieved by a positive attitude. They see it as a key differentiator between them and other organizations. Working flexibly is a thing that matters, so it should be seen as normal.

Introduction

Mobile working is not just giving mobile workers mobile devices and sending them off to do their job. It often requires an e-engineering of business processes and implementation of new management practices to support mobile workers. Without due attention to managerial aspects, mobile working is unlikely to result in the desired business benefits. This chapter will cover management challenges and operational issues in mobile working. The main focus will be on what managerial issues arise when managing mobile working operations. Some suggestions for dealing with these issues will also be included.

Mobile working: key issues

Having discussed various aspects of mobile working in the previous chapters, this section presents some of the key issues in managing mobile working effectively.

Management structures for mobile working

Many businesses that have embraced mobile working say they are reaping the benefits but they have learned that mobile working needs a change in management style, with an emphasis on good communication and rigorous measurement of performance (Antony, 2004). Middle managers could lose their jobs if they lack the skills to manage teams of mobile workers. Mobile working will mean that managers will have to trust their staff more and move away from the traditional controlling style of management (Silicon, 2005). This also involves coaching and motivating employees to be responsible, independent and yet stay a part of teams responsible for delivery of certain tasks.

Ability of company IT infrastructure to cope with mobile working and security demands

Mobile technologies are evolving quickly but many security and infrastructure issues remain unaddressed. Mobile computing users link to the network in many different ways including Wireless WANs and LANs, Wireless Personal Area Networks (PANs), ad hoc networks, cellular, satellite, and infrared (Kentrick, 2002). In some cases where costs or coverage are a limiting factor, the handheld devices store data and then synchronize it with a laptop via a serial cable or cradle (Pascoe, 2002).

In wireless networks, the server can store data instead of the client, which frees up computing resources in the mobile device. Wireless connections also allow asynchronous real time integration and update with the database as well as utilizing real time data mining from multiple sources (Barbash, 2001). Wireless data architecture, however, still comes with its own set of issues. On the network side, these include limited bandwidth, unreliable connections, questionable security and a lack of a single connectivity standard. On the hardware side, these issues include lack of storage capacity in devices, small screen sizes and limited memory (Barbash, 2001). Continuous advances in technology have improved things and will continue to do so in the future.

Many enterprises are uncertain of the various options they may have due to the emerging nature of mobile computing technologies. Additionally, they are concerned about the integration of mobile technologies with existing IT infrastructure and applications (Minder 2004). Some organizations try to extend their existing remote access VPN solution to devices that connect wirelessly. Early adopters have reported that this approach falls short of expectations. Reasons are numerous, including poor performance on wireless WANs, the inconvenience and latency associated with repeated login after loss of connectivity and application session disruption when roaming both within and beyond any given wireless network (Phifer, 2004). This implies that if users are to have seamless mobility for their remote access connections, the technologies described in this article must be accompanied by business arrangements among different network owners, as is the case today in cellular voice networks (Phifer, 2004).

Accessibility issues

High speed public Internet access is offering opportunities to get, and stay, connected in more locations. Today, hotels that cater to business travellers frequently offer in-room high speed Internet access. As these high speed access networks ramp up, mobile workers are changing their habits, remaining online for longer (Phifer, 2004). It may take several years to reach that 'always connected' goal, and connectivity in less populous areas will lag behind high tech corridors.

Acceptance issues

The user acceptance of technology is another major issue. There are many problems that have slowed the adoption of mobile computing. One problem is that mobile technology still lags significantly behind desktop computing in terms of processing power, power availability and network speed. Additionally, the rapidly changing pace of mobile computing has reduced the ability for business professionals to keep up with, understand, and utilize the available technology (York and Pendharkar, 2004). Another concern is whether or not future technology will meet user demands (Kentrick, 2002).

Human Computer Interface (HCI) issues are also a key area in technology acceptance. HCI includes the use and context of computers, human characteristics, computer systems, and interface architecture and the development process. By understanding the nature of the circumstances and problems mobile workers face and the possible resources available to resolve their issues, designers and developers are better able to respond to their needs. Touch screen technologies have made the interfaces easier to use but they are still a long way off the goal of usability in all conditions.

HCI issues in mobile working are different in the mobile working context than in the traditional office environment. Kristoffersen (1999) identifies four key elements that define mobile work contexts and explains how they differ from the office setting:

- Tasks external to operating the mobile computer are the most important, as opposed to tasks taking place in the computer (e.g. a spreadsheet for an office worker).
- Users' hands are often used to manipulate physical objects, as opposed to users in the traditional office setting, whose hands are safely and ergonomically placed on the keyboard.
- Users may be involved in tasks (outside the computer) that demand a high level of visual attention (to avoid danger as well as monitor progress), as opposed to the traditional office setting where a large degree of visual attention is usually directed at the computer.
- Users may be highly mobile during the task, as opposed to in the office. Their conditions such as lighting, sitting space, etc., are also different from traditional office settings.

Mobile workers are typically both producers and users of corporate data as they access systems for information and input observation or customer data from the field. This can take various forms including dispatch services, work order management and enterprise communications. Methods to ease the burden of input and spread the requirements of processing output over all the human senses, while still maintaining data integrity, are of high importance (York and Pendharkar, 2004). Speech and handwriting recognition are two growing forms of input. The benefits of speech recognition include minimal user attention input, direct system entry, remote microphone capabilities and a faster speed of operation compared to other competing input methods, but its usability in noisy environments and unreliability in terms of accuracy of input are the main drawbacks.

Is it productive?

Many articles claim that mobile working increases productivity. For example, a recent article at Silicon.com (2005) claimed that the key benefit of mobility is not based on a binary decision to 'work on the move' or not. Having the option and ability to occasionally 'work on the move' is the key. The technology allows for a flexible choice of where we work and this is what gives the productivity benefits. Research carried out earlier this year for Blackberry maker RIM, by Ipsos Reid, came to the conclusion that employers can recuperate 188 working hours a year, which is equal to a month of work assuming a maximum of 48 hour working week. To an executive on £100,000 a year, that translates to £9,800 in annual recovered downtime which is an attractive proposition to any company (Hallett, 2004). Similar research, carried out by the Economist Intelligence Unit found that mobility friendly companies have more productive employees. This refers to the use of mobile technology, rather than saying workers should all get out on the road more, and a key finding was that those who do have to travel a lot are desperate for good technology. That's not quite the same thing as, say, extending a mainly deskbound worker's day by having them answering emails on the way to and from the office or at the weekend (Hallett, 2004). Having said that, many (see Chapter 2) also question mobile working's promise of high productivity and more research is needed to address this issue.

Work/life balance debate

Though mobile working has been promoted as a way to increase efficiency, particularly for frequent travellers, it also lengthens the working day by turning commuting time, as well as evenings and weekends, into productive time. The intrusive nature of an 'always on' culture has its downsides too. Research has consistently shown that those who work from home put in longer hours than they would if they had been in the office (Carr, 2005). Some now even take their mobile work devices such as tablets or smart phones with them on holidays and regularly check or respond to their emails.

Commuting and the old nine-to-five desk-based existence may well be stressful but we also need to think more carefully about how we are going to maintain worker's well being in this 'always on' corporate culture (Silicon.com 2004). Studies show that home workers, for example, end up putting in more hours than their office-based counterparts, albeit often willingly so, but with little attention paid to health and safety standards (Hallett, 2004). Workers are overloaded with information and many already feel overly available (Wirelessnews, 2004). Almost half of mobile workers feel alienated from office life, underappreciated and mistrusted, according to a study by IBM and the Economist Intelligence Unit. The study of 351 mobile workers in 29 European countries revealed that 40 per cent felt disadvantaged because they could not tap into 'water cooler' conversations and informal office networking (McCue, 2005).

With home-based workers, isolation is always an issue. Do they feel like part of the team? One may have to factor in time to make people feel like part of the group (Stedman, 2004). A study showed that the majority of mobile workers said they did not believe their company properly advocated mobile and flexible working (Silicon.com, 2005).

The answer to these problems may be balance (Silicon.com, 2005). Most businesses will keep the office space and maintain teams working in one location as much as possible while allowing those workers who know and see each other regularly to take advantage of mobile working on a sporadic basis. This might change however and the balance may keep shifting towards more and more time away from the set offices.

Individual and organizational benefits/drawbacks

As discussed earlier in this chapter, mobile working has its benefits, such as increased productivity and flexibility for workers who can enjoy benefits such as avoiding long commutes or popping out to the doctor's or the bank during working hours because the boss can still contact them. However it is no holy grail. People have talked about running 'virtual offices' in the future with no central location. Instead, colleagues work from home and on the road and rarely see each other in person (Silicon.com, 2005). Business is by nature collaborative and the more communication technologies advance, the more we're coming to appreciate just how good the face-to-face paradigm is (Silicon.com, 2005). Mobile devices can also be difficult to use and manage. Managing these benefits and drawbacks is one of the key issues in mobile working.

Chapter summary

This chapter was a discussion of key technical, social, operational and strategic issues in mobile working. These included the arguments and counter arguments about the effects of mobile working on work life balance, performance/productivity gains, technology acceptance, human computer interaction, new working patterns acceptance, benefits/drawbacks of mobile working and limitations in current mobile technology.

4

MOBILE TECHNOLOGIES

Case study: United Utilities

This case study was prepared by the author to facilitate class discussion rather than illustrate effective or ineffective management practices. Only publicly available material has been used to write this case and it does not reflect any opinions of employees or management at this organization.

United Utilities PLC was created from the merger of North West Water and Norweb in November 1995. Its principal activities are managing and operating the regulated electricity distribution, water and wastewater networks in North West England, a region with a population of around 7 million. At United Utilities, the current system is limited to its clean water side. Calls are sent via a call centre, which logs information and generates a work order if a visit is required. The network controllers in the field have laptops in their vans on which they download their work assignments and upload information once they have finished on site. They can see what work the network controller (who works from home) has got throughout the day. Network controllers also have plans on their laptops of all mains records, so they have got access not just to their own area but if they are doing emergency cover for surrounding areas, they have the information for them too. This means they don't have to send out the person that usually does that area.

Emergency jobs are communicated via mobile phones and added to the work list on the laptop on an ongoing basis. The next time the field worker logs in, the additional work is downloaded on to the system. At the moment United Utilities' system is limited to network controllers, whose task is to identify leakage problems rather than rectify them, meaning that the more complex areas of spares availability and the need to make contact with depots to pick up parts has been thus far avoided.

One of United Utilities' network controllers confirmed that field staff are happy with the system.

> It is convenient. With the paper system we used to have to go into the office in the morning and get our work, and go in at the end of the day so that someone could put it on the system.

With a laptop, there is no need for him to go in other than for meetings and to provide paperwork for non-connected depots. He says it works well: 'We very rarely have problems. Sometimes with the computer when one comes to pick up work, there's nothing there, but I can't remember the last time that happened. It's a really good system.'

The current system is near the end of its usable life. United Utilities is working on a new concept, Connect, which will replace it. According to Sally Ainsworth, Business Delivery Manager for Connect, the plan is to roll out Connect to other areas of the business too, such as waste water and electricity. At the moment, the company's electricity business works in a very traditional way, in and out of depots using a shift system. But the advent of Connect should change all this. The new 'ruggedized' notebook PCs will use broadband, so as information becomes available at the call centre it will also appear on the field laptop, eliminating the need to upload or download information (Stedman, 2004).

Introduction

Technological advancements in mobile communications are happening rapidly. This chapter will cover technologies of the past, present and near future, together with suggestions for choosing the right technologies to meet business objectives as well as selecting the right suppliers. It will address the evolution of mobile working technologies and their typical uses, providing a foundation for the rest of the text, but seeing the technologies throughout as enabling mechanisms to the mobile-working-related organizational and human issues.

It will describe the common ICT systems, systems architectures and middleware in use. It will cover technological trends in the past and indicates the possible future directions and implications. Some mobile technologies including mobile devices, interface issues and technical infrastructure required to support smooth functioning of mobile equipment will also be discussed.

The Internet

The emergence of the Internet has posed a host of new opportunities and organizational challenges, both technological and managerial (Teo and Too, 2000). Given the Internet's potential to revolutionize business operations especially from a mobile working perspective, it is very important to understand the nature and implications of the Internet.

The Internet is a massive global network of interconnected packet-switched computer networks. Hoffman (2002) offers three (mutually consistent) definitions of the Internet: a network of networks based on the TCP/IP protocols; a community of people who use and develop those networks; and a collection of resources that can be reached from those networks.

The most exciting commercial developments are occurring on that portion of the Internet known as the World Wide Web (WWW). The WWW is a distributed hypermedia environment within the Internet, which was originally developed by the European Particle Physics Laboratory (CERN). Global hypermedia allows multimedia information to be located on a network of servers around the world, which are interconnected, allowing navigation through the information by clicking on hyperlinks. Any hyperlink (text, icon or image in a document) can point to any document anywhere on the Internet. Most mobile devices use these internet technologies.

The homepages of the WWW utilize the system of hyperlinks to simplify the task of navigating among the offerings on the Internet. These attributes enable the Web to be an efficient channel for advertising, marketing and even direct distribution of certain goods and information services. Rapid developments in this area have resulted in the introduction of later versions of the web with ever enhancing interactivity and functionality. These developments have made the Internet cost effective and the quickest platform for mobile working.

Internet technology can make a significant contribution to a company's value chain. It can improve a company's relationship with vendors and suppliers, its internal operations and its customer relations, and offers the prospect of reaching a rapidly expanding user base. The Internet also resulted in dramatically lower communications costs by eliminating obstacles created by geography, time zones and locations so it can be said that it is one of the key catalysts for the development of mobile working.

Evolution of mobile technologies

Mobile technologies are one of the fastest to evolve in terms of development and adoption. As presented in Table 4.1, within a few decades, mobile devices have evolved from just a concept to multi functional business tools. Table 4.2 suggests the significant improvements of mobile technology has happened at an astonishing speed and present mobile phone users are approaching billions, growing faster than ever.

Mobile devices such as Personal Digital Assistants (PDAs) and mobile phones are in widespread use already today and converging to mobile smart phones and tablets. They enable the users to access a wide range of services and information. Not so long ago, wireless communications were very limited with regards to functionality of devices and speed of communications. Constraints such as screen size, memory and storage capabilities as well as data transfer rates limited the amount of data that could be both displayed and accessed.

With recent advancements in wireless data transfer, such as GPRS and 4G (4th Generation) services, data transmission speeds mirror and will eventually exceed that of current landline-based connections. As networks increase their speed, this allows

TABLE 4.1 Evolution of mobile technologies from mobile working perspective

Year	Name of Technology	Uses
1940s–Present	Cell radio	Emergency vehicles, taxis, etc.
1973	1st Mobile phone	For use by individuals in a limited geographic area
1979	1st Cellular network in Japan	Long distance mass communication
1980	Automated cellular network in Japan	Long distance mass communication
1983	First generation (1G) was introduced by Motorola	Voice communication between several countries
1990	Second-generation wireless telephone technology (2G) introduced in Finland	Voice as well as text communication (SMS)
1980–1994	Development of GSM	Location-based communications
1997	1st Mobile Phone games	Entertainment
2000	3G first launched in Japan + Camera phones	For voice, text, multimedia messaging and online browsing
2001–	Features such as calendars, mp3 players, notepad, etc. + PDAs	For personal and business use
2003–	Smart phones with multiple functions useful for businesses	Many productivity tools such as word processing, data capture, analysis, etc.

more opportunity and feasibility for mobile computing applications. Similarly, as the costs of handheld computing devices and connectivity fall, their use becomes more viable for business operations. As advances in technology increase coverage, data speeds and usability, greater user acceptance will fuel development of new applications that are more useful for businesses in the maturing mobile computing environment.

While the current industry standard for mobile phones is 3G or 3rd generation, in 2011 Apple released its already-iconic iPhone 5 which boasts 4G capabilities, and the HTC corporation have released their own 4G model. However, even though these phones have 4G capabilities, network transmission in many countries is not sufficient or yet up to speed. In reality, therefore, the latest handsets cannot always be used to their full potential because they are not supported by adequate network infrastructure and because good coverage, even in advanced countries, is still a long way off.

After considerable confusion about definitions, The International Telecommunications Union (ITU) announced in a press statement of November 2010 that 'two technologies can now be counted as 4G, LTE-Advanced and WirelessMAN-Advanced' and went on to describe 4G as providing:

> A global platform on which to build the next-generations of interactive mobile services that will provide faster data access, enhanced roaming capabilities, unified messaging and broadband multimedia.
>
> *(ITU, cited in O'Sullivan, 2010)*

	FDMA		
	Mobitex		
	NMT		
	TACS		
2G	CDMA	Up to 20Kbps	• Digital voice service
	GSM		• Push-to-Talk (PTT)
	iDEN		• Short Message Service (SMS)
			• Conference calling
	PCS		• Caller ID
	TDMA		• Voice mail
			• Simple data applications such as email and Web browsing
2.5G	CDMA2000 1xRTT	Up to 144Kbps (typical 60-80Kbps)	All 2G features plus: • MMS (Multimedia Message Service)
	GPRS	Up to 114Kbps (30-40Kbps)	• Web browsing • Real-time location-based services such as directions
	HSCSD	Up to 64Kbps	Basic multimedia, including support for short audio and video clips, games and images
	EDGE	Up to 384Kbps	
	WiDEN	Up to 100Kbps	
2.75G	EGPRS 2	473Kbps (uplink) to 1.2Mbps (downlink)[2]	Better performance for all 2/2.5G services
3G (DSL speeds)	CDMA2000 EVDO (data only) Rev 0	Up to 2.4Mbps	Support for all 2G and 2.5G features plus: • Full motion video
	CDMA2000 EVDV (simultaneous voice and data)	Up to 2.4Mbps	• Streaming music • 3D gaming • Faster Web browsing
	UMTS	Up to 2Mbps	
	WCDMA	Up to 2Mbps	
	CDMA2000/ EVDO-Rev A	Up to 3.1Mbps	
3.5G (cable speeds)	HSDPA	Up to 14.4Mbps	Support for all 2/2.5/3G features plus:
	CDMA2000/ EVDO Rev B	Up to 46Mbps	• On-demand video • Video conferencing • Faster Web browsing (especially graphics intensive sites)
4G (wired networking equivalent)	WiMAX	100+Mbps	Support for all prior 2G/3G features plus:
	UMB	35Mbps	• High quality streaming video • High quality videoconferencing
	LTE	100Mbps	• High quality Voice-over-IP (VoIP)

TABLE 4.2 Cellular network generation (Motorola, 2008)

While there is an ongoing debate in the telecommunications industry as to which technology will become the industry standard, it is widely accepted, and predicted, that these are the two technologies which are most likely to provide the speeds needed for mobile working. LTE or long-term evolution is more of a natural progression from the 3rd generation technologies already in widespread use, such as GSM, whereas WiMAX is based on a different platform altogether. Both of the technologies are IP based, which means that they transfer data over the internet rather than by voice, telephonically, but LTE still uses SIM-card technology and operates through a mobile network similar to that of 3G handsets. WiMAX, on the other hand, operates in a manner similar to WiFi in that it works by connecting to base stations. One of the most significant advantages LTE has over WiMAX is that it is possible to operate LTE over pre-existing networks whereas WiMAX will require the construction of entirely new networks, as the old and new technologies are not compatible. It is for this reason that LTE is the technology currently being trial tested in Scandinavia and South Korea (Syputa, 2009).

South Korea is one of the few countries claiming to have a national network capable of delivering full 4G speeds which purport to be up to 40 times faster than the 4G networks that are currently standard in the UK. Indeed, the promotional website www.thaivisa.com enthusiastically proclaims that:

> The system allows users to view high-definition, three-dimensional TV images while in a car moving 40 kilometers per hour and transmit 600 megabits of data per second (Mbps), which enables a regular 700 megabyte CD to be downloaded in 9.3 seconds. It is also six times faster than the LTE or 3.9 generation.
>
> *(Thaivisa, 2010)*

This confidence is well-founded as some East Asian states have invested heavily in order to secure the frontier of developments in mobile technologies as a means of exploiting mobile working and m-commerce. However, until the level of investment required for this generation of network platforms is repeated across the globe, naturally there will tend to be reluctance to adopt mobile working in those countries where lower levels of investment have resulted in weak mobile infrastructures. If increased speed and reliability of network connections such as those demonstrated by the South Korean system are achieved, it would bring about widespread use of mobile working. A new generation of technologies or 'tech savvy' workers is not, in itself, enough to drive the mobile working forward at a desired pace. Rather, it is the network infrastructure delivery systems developed by countries such as South Korea and Scandinavia that will provide the essential platform.

Sweden and Norway have developed 4G LTE networks in Stockholm and Oslo. Although the speed of the networks (approximately 100 megabits per second in 2009) does not match those of South Korea, they are nonetheless still far superior to 3G networks, and it is worth noting that the Scandinavian network has been in place longer than that of South Korea and is scheduled to improve speeds in the near future. In some instances, no handsets capable of connecting directly to the infrastructure were available, so connection was only possible via broadband dongles through a laptop. However, new generation of smart phones are now able to access these networks.

It should also be noted here that there are currently two forms of LTE technology available: LTE Advanced and LTE 3GPP. LTE Advanced is simply a progression from LTE3 GPP and will have some extra functions which were not possible on LTE 3GPP including: Worldwide functionality and roaming compatibility of services; interworking with other radio access systems; enhanced peak data rates to support advanced services and applications, etc. These added features make advanced LTE the obvious choice of countries who are looking to upgrade their existing networks to make sure they will be capable of supporting 4G technologies.

If we now turn to the hardware, it is clear that the application of smart phone technology embodies some of the essential characteristics of a computer, such as the readiness to connect to the internet. Although 3G networks have been operational since 2000, the model and make of smart phone which is generally acknowledged as the industry standard of comparable quality and matched to 3G infrastructures is the Apple iPhone. The iPhone was released onto the market at the beginning of 2007 followed quickly by a HTC touch phone. The vastly improved data speeds provided by 3G phones have made accessing the Internet much more practicable from mobile phones. In addition, other key features such as GPS-enabled mobile phones allow the user to access the internet using search engines such as Google, and where results will be displayed in order of their proximity in addition to other location-based services.

As well as reviewing the development of mobile technology to date, from first to fourth generations, some observers have already talking about fifth generation (5G) devices that will facilitate significantly increased bandwidth on mobile devices, capable of data speeds and bandwidth equivalent to those achievable in homes or offices. Importantly, this extension of technical facility via mobile technologies will permit users to access high-speed and high-capacity broadband connections on their mobile devices.

Mobile devices

There are many different types of devices used for mobile working. This section summarises (see Table 4.3) some of the most common mobile working devices. They are not always direct competitors as they have different features and are suited to different uses. Some, like Bluetooth, work in tandem with other devices covered in this section.

TABLE 4.3 Some common devices and their key features

Mobile Device	Key Features
PDAs **(Handhelds,** **Pocket PCs)**	Wireless modem. Access via cellular networks to the Internet, company applications, email, instant messaging, etc.
Laptop	Smaller version of a PC, with a flat screen and keyboard in one portable package. Using a mobile phone, most laptops can connect to the Internet. This can be done without any cabling by using Bluetooth or WiFi.
Tablet PC	Combines laptop, planners, calendars, notebooks and handheld devices like PDAs into a single device. Suitable for knowledge intensive work.
GPRS Device	The technology that supports most current mobile phones, allowing access e-mail and the Internet on the move. Suited to sending and receiving small bursts of data, such as email and web browsing.
Bluetooth	A way of instantly connecting up electronic devices. Can talk to any other device provided it is in range (usually 10m, but this can be up to 100m for some equipment).
Smartphone	Combination of cellular phone and PDA. Access and transmission of data using existing cellular networks. Conventional phone functions and endless other features.

Smart phones

Smart phones are a combination of cellular phone and PDA, which enable access and transmission of data using existing cellular networks. Conventional phone functions, wireless email, internet browsing, fax, personal information management, LAN connectivity, data entry, local data transfer between phone and computers, remote data transfer and remote control of electronic home or business systems.

Smart phones came in two waves, 3G stands for third generation and 4G for fourth generation. The key thing about these phones is the features they offer, including:

- they are permanently connected, so, unlike Wireless Access Protocol (WAP) phones, there is no waiting time to access the Web. They also have a much higher data transfer rate;
- much more functionality through apps;
- the ability to connect with a variety of platforms and systems; and
- easy-to-use interfaces for a variety of uses and users.

The key feature driving the sales of these phones has been speedier data transmission speed which allows owners to watch streamed video clips such as goals from football matches or to hold video calls with other users. While the quality may not be good enough to make it a replacement for formal meetings, it is certainly a useful communication tool. These phones also come with a range of other useful options such as digital cameras, web and email access, the ability to play music and video files as well as a wide range of other applications. There are millions of applications available to perform a variety of tasks. It is suitable for people who need to be constantly contactable, but do not need the features of a PDA or laptop, such as some engineers or other field workers. Table 4.4 indicates the main operating platforms in the market from 2011 and the forecast of market share in 2015. It seems that PDA devices will occupy Android and this operating system will dominate the market share in the following years.

TABLE 4.4 2011–2015 worldwide smartphone operating system market share compound annual growth rate (IDC, 2011)

Operating System	2011 Market Share	2015 Market Share	2011–2015 Unit CAGR
Android	38.9%	43.8%	23.7%
BlackBerry OS	14.2%	13.4%	18.3%
Symbian	20.6%	0.1%	-68.8%
iOS	18.2%	16.9%	17.9%
Windows Phone 7/Windows Mobile	3.8%	20.3%	82.3%
Others	4.3%	5.5%	27.6%
Total	100.0%	100.0%	20.1%

PDAs

PDA stands for Personal Digital Assistant. Also known as 'palmtops'; these handheld devices have an increasing amount of power and are far more than just electronic diaries. Most PDAs now run versions of standard office software which means one can work on documents, spreadsheets or other files from the office. Cheaper PDAs need to be connected to the network so that they can 'synchronise' themselves and download any new files like emails that have arrived and upload any files one may have worked on while away from the desk. Increasingly, though, PDAs are available with 'Bluetooth' and 'WiFi' options, which allow them to access a network wirelessly. Many PDAs also double as mobile phones and can be linked to laptops for wireless Internet access.

The main benefits of PDAs include their small size, light weight, low price and compatibility with common office software and other tools such as Bluetooth and WiFi. Their small screen and keyboards however make them unattractive for some users. PDAs are ideal for people who are rarely at their desk, dealing with email, scheduling, making notes and reviewing documents on the move.

Laptop

A laptop is a smaller version of a Personal Computer (PC), with a flat screen and keyboard in one portable package. As computers get more powerful and memory becomes cheaper, laptops have become smaller, more affordable and more powerful. Many businesses have replaced desktop computers altogether, giving employees laptops which can be plugged in to docking stations to connect to networks and recharge their batteries. These advances mean that laptops can do almost anything that a desktop PC can. Using a mobile phone, most laptops can connect to the Internet. Increasingly, this can be done without any cabling by using Bluetooth or WiFi (explained later in this section).

Laptops have a full keyboard, reasonable size screen, a lot of processing power and large storage space which makes them a more attractive option than PDAs; however their relatively larger size, expensive parts and upgrades and limited battery life can count against them. Laptops are ideal for presentations, hot-desking, staff travelling between sites and working from home, etc.

Although some of the newer laptop PCs come with built in 3G, or ports which allow you to install 3G SIM-cards, thereby making it possible to connect to the internet via mobile networks, connection is also achievable by using a dongle, a piece of hardware which connects to a USB port in a laptop. Dongles are popular, not only because they allow users to connect to the internet whilst they are out of the reach of a wireless point, but also because they often operate on a 'pay as you go' basis. Obviously, this enables people without fixed incomes, who cannot afford contracts, to connect to the internet via mobile networks and not be faced with a bill for broadband internet access. However, dongles may yet be superseded in some areas by the sheer number of smart phones in the market which can often be used to connect laptops to the internet by means of a USB lead in much of the same way as a dongle does. However, dongles do have a loyal customer base, and all transactions which are made through laptops connected to the internet in this way are still classified as mobile transactions, so they are contributing to the use of mobile working.

Tablet PC

Tablet PCs, such as the iPad and Surface, are specifically designed as mobile computers. The Tablet PC combines laptop, planners, calendars, notebooks and handheld devices like PDAs into a single device, thereby replacing the range of electronic and paper-based resources that knowledge workers typically need to carry. By capturing and storing the full history of personal files, notes and records in digital form and providing full mobile access to the corporate systems, Tablet PCs create a new capability for knowledge workers to immediately have all the resources they would normally have at their office desk to hand regardless of location (Garfinkel, 2004). Tablet PCs are a very useful tool for many mobile knowledge workers but numerous features may be unnecessary for most of them.

Tablets which can be described as a hybrid, something between a smart phone and a laptop computer, with the attributes of each. There have been many previous attempts to develop touch screen tablet computers, or PDF devices that could only connect to the Internet via a wireless connection and have never proved to be popular. The iPad, however, comes in various models, one which is only able to connect to the internet via a Wi-Fi network, and another which comes with a 3G connection via a range of network providers – hybrid tablet-smartphones, with any transactions coming through 3G connections classed as mobile commerce. The obvious advantage of tablets, both for the consumers and the industry is that although tablets are still portable, unlike mobile phones they have a much bigger screen so there is no need for modified user interfaces as is sometimes the case with mobile phones. They also come with long battery life, often enough for days of use.

Due to the success of the iPad tablet there have been many similar versions of this technology released by other companies such as Samsung, all of whom are competing for a share of what is being seen as a rapidly emerging market. Gartner (2011) forecasts sales estimates for the tablet market until 2015, illustrated as Table 4.5, which believes Apple will maintain the lead market share with more than 50% until 2014. Milanesi (2011) argues this is because of the superior and unified user experience across the hardware, software and services that Apple provides. To challenge the Apple's position, competitors need to respond with a similar approach to fulfil customer experience.

GPRS Device

General Packet Radio Service (GPRS) is the technology that supports most current mobile phones, allowing access to email and the Internet on the move. With data transfer rates of up to 171KBPS, GPRS devices are particularly suited to sending and

TABLE 4.5 Tablet market share forecast (Gartner, 2011)

OS	2010	2011	2012	2015
Android	2,512	11,020	22,875	116,444
iOS	14,685	46,697	69,025	148,674
MeeGo	179	476	490	197
Microsoft	0	0	4,348	34,435
QNX	0	3,016	6,274	26,123
WebOS	0	2,053	0	0
Others	235	375	467	431
Total	**17,610**	**63,637**	**103,479**	**326,304**

receiving small bursts of data, such as email and web browsing. As well as voice calls and text messages, they often support multimedia messaging (messages containing a combination of text, sounds, images and video). Many GPRS mobile phone providers offer an integration service, linking a company email system to mobile handsets.

This device can connect to laptops to provide Internet access for mobile working. It is fairly cheap, widely available and easy to use. Its drawbacks are that it is slower than 3G phones and no video calling functions are available. It is ideal for mobile communication such as checking emails on the move, rather than full mobile working. GPRS is a standard feature on the majority of current mobile phones so there are no extra equipment costs in most cases.

Bluetooth

Bluetooth is a way of instantly connecting up electronic devices. Using radio waves, any Bluetooth enabled device can talk to any other device provided it is in range (usually 10 meters, but this can be up to 100 meters for some equipment). Bluetooth is best thought of as a way of creating ad hoc networks for consumer devices. So for example: a Bluetooth enabled laptop could print straight to a Bluetooth enabled printer without a cabled connection, a PDA could automatically synchronise itself with a PC just by being in the office and a mobile phone could be used to connect a laptop to the Internet.

The potential benefits include: one no longer needs a phone or network connecter to access the Internet with a laptop; meeting rooms can become cable free; and visitors to an office can simply sit at a desk and begin working. Finally, an increasing number of electrical devices are now Bluetooth compatible or can be upgraded with cards or adaptors, which means that Bluetooth can be used without substantial extra investment.

Drawbacks include short range and not being robust enough to replace a standard wired network in an office. It is suitable for connecting up disparate electronic items in companies with limited IT budgets. Bluetooth technology is increasingly built into contemporary mobile phones, PDAs, PCs and PC-related products. If not, a Bluetooth adaptor or card for many devices can be purchased.

Now the question arises, 'what are the key hardware requirements for mobile workers. While it is difficult to generalize across all mobile work situations, Pascoe (2002) provides a list of hardware criteria for fieldworkers:

- Pen user interfaces provide a natural substitute for paper-based systems. They are also more suitable to the mobile environment compared to miniature keyboards.
- The device should not adversely affect the user's body or senses.
- Battery life should be substantial enough to last for an entire workday without requiring a recharge.
- Devices should be robust enough to withstand dropping and environmental conditions of the workplace. There are options for ruggedized equipment, but it is often available at a considerable price.
- The device should support connectivity to multiple sensor devices, equipment and networks.

Having described some of the main attributes of mobile devices and solutions summarized in Table 4.1. It would be useful to know which of these are in practical use. In a survey done by Newsweek (Wirelessnews, 2004), mobile workers identified more than twenty different communication tools and devices that are used on a regular basis at work, at home and on the road. On average, workers say they regularly juggle about seven different communication tools for work: work phone, work email, personal email, work fax machine, personal mobile phone, home phone and work voicemail (Wirelessnews, 2004). This means a combined solution such as 'ubicomp' will be welcomed by the mobile workers. Ubicomp solutions typically include input and output (I/O) functionality that mirrors the way humans communicate such as speaking, gesturing and writing (Branco, 2001).

Ubicomp solutions typically involve using context awareness in a device as both an input function and to control output modes (York and Pendharkar, 2004). In these types of solutions, the device ergonomics considerations are important in fostering the natural 'fit' of machines to human interaction. Invisible interaction with machines based on their contextual perception and natural human communication forms is most likely to be adopted rapidly in areas such as some forms of mobile working where traditional GUI interfaces are not appropriate (Crowley, Coutaz and Berard, 2000).

Ubicomp is relevant to mobile workers whose use of computing power is generally secondary to the task at hand (e.g. an emergency field health care worker who needs to attend to a patient while collecting data for the admitting hospital). The goals of Ubicomp can be summarized as follows:

- everyday human tasks must be understood and supported by an appropriate interaction experience (York and Pendharkar, 2004);
- heterogeneous solutions should be available to offer differing forms of interactive experience as situations warrant (York and Pendharkar, 2004);
- these solutions, when networked, should provide a holistic user experience (Abowd, 2002).

A traditional GUI interface often demands too many visual and cognitive resources to be practical for mobile computing, since human interaction with the machine is generally secondary to the task at hand. Because of these issues, it is important that we consider ubicomp solutions for mobile computing in a variable work context (York and Pendharkar, 2004). The solutions, however, are far from their promised functionality and are not widely available yet so alternatives such as future Tablet PCs may offer a solution to device inter-connectivity problems.

Network solutions

There are many networking solutions which are suitable for different requirements such as network size, speed required and geographical area covered. This section covers some of the most common networking solutions (Summarized in Table 4.6) available for organizations engaged in mobile working.

WiFi

WiFi is the name for a group of standards that govern how wireless networks operate. It is the default setup for most wireless technologies from wireless Internet access in coffee shops to wireless broadband in rural areas. Like Bluetooth, a large number of mobile devices are WiFi compatible. It can be used to network whole offices and provide Internet access ('hotspots') almost anywhere, even outside a building. Its main advantages include wide availability, Internet access anywhere there is a WiFi network and high speed, and most devices are simple to use.

Prices of WiFi networks are falling but it is still quite expensive and requires some technical expertise to set up a network. WiFi is ideal for traveling workers, hot-desking, non-desk-based staff such as warehouse workers, businesses with limited space or those who want to create cable-free offices. Typically, a wireless access point can cover up to 100 meters and support up to 256 users, depending on the specification of the equipment. WiFi hotspots have been growing quickly around the world with many cafes, restaurants, hotels, airports, trains, coaches, etc., offering WiFi hotspots.

TABLE 4.6 Mobile working network solutions

Network	Description
Wifi	A group of standards that govern how wireless networks operate. Can be used to network whole offices and provide Internet access ('hotspots') almost anywhere.
Extranets	A way of giving people access to business information using an Internet browser. A private network which enables sharing specified areas of information or operations with people such as clients, customers, suppliers or staff.
Virtual Private Network (VPN)	A secure way to give remote access to a network to other offices or individuals. Uses the Internet and encryption technology.

Extranets

An Extranet is a way of giving people access to business information using an Internet browser. It is a private network which enables sharing specified areas of information or operations with people like clients, customers, suppliers or staff. At its simplest level, an Extranet can be a password protected area on the company's website. At the top end, it can be a very sophisticated way of sharing product and pricing data; accepting orders and payments and managing collaborative projects online. A company may allow different people to access different levels and types of information.

It is a relatively low-cost option which allows files to be transferred which are too big to be emailed. It makes it easier for mobile workers to access company data or extend this access to clients and other supply chain partners. Once of the main drawbacks is that extranets are not directly linked to the company network, so files have to be uploaded to it, which means users are not necessarily working with the most up-to-date information. Extranet security is also an issue so it may not be suitable for highly confidential information.

Virtual Private Network

A Virtual Private Network (VPN) is a secure way to give remote access to a network to other offices or individuals. Unlike systems for linking offices through privately leased phone lines, a VPN uses the Internet and encryption technology. This means it is very secure, widely accessible and cheaper than leased lines. They are also very flexible so users can access the network anytime, which means they always have the most current data. It is also quick and easy to give access to new users and create virtual teams.

VPNs require investment in new equipment and technical knowledge which many not be available to some companies. They are suitable for businesses with a set of permanent mobile or home workers, or several offices who work collaboratively on confidential projects with business partners for whom data security is a prime consideration. Most VPN options require a broadband connection and have installation and annual charges.

The question of which of the previously described (or other) solutions (that typically look like the process presented in Figure 4.1), an organization may use, depends on a number of factors such as budget, security/technical/business requirements and availability of relevant resources. In terms of future developments, the Internet has established itself as a communication and service medium of choice for many. Current and next generation wireless communication technologies (e.g. WiFi and or VPNs) are likely to foster the penetration of the Internet towards mobile use via a broad range of devices.

Connectivity applications

As discussed in the previous two sections, a typical mobile worker may have several devices such as work phone, mobile phone, voicemail, email, PDA or a Laptop.

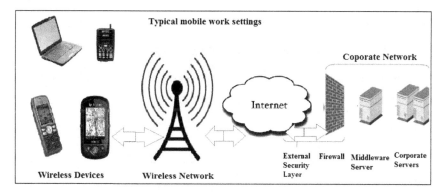

FIGURE 4.1 Typical mobile work settings

Despite myriad communication tools and devices available in today's enterprise environment, many workers are still dissatisfied with their ability to reach colleagues and obtain critical information when needed. With so many tools to choose from, workers'·top communication complaints include:

- must leave multiple messages in different places when seeking immediate responses;
- malfunctions while travelling or working mobile;
- inability to access timely and accurate information due to redundant back-end systems and out-of-date information;
- inability to respond to a missed client call in a timely manner due to environmental factors such as travelling in noisy trains or being in crowded places;
- lack of synchronization among various communication tools.

There are many mobile working applications available in the market, which help integrate various communication devices and enterprise systems to help overcome some of the problems mentioned above. Mainly, there are two main enterprise mobility mechanisms to reach the goal, namely mobile groupware applications and mobile enterprise applications. The mobile groupware application is developed for convenient communication via the web and in some cases integrated with enterprise applications.

Mobile groupware application

Groupware was first known in 1980 and it enables users located remotely from each other to work collaboratively on related tasks via a network (e.g. LAN and WAN). Most groupware products (e.g. Lotus Notes, Microsoft Exchange) include a messaging system, document sharing and management software, a calendaring and scheduling system for coordinating meetings and tracking the progress of group projects, electronic conferencing and an electronic newsletter (Webster's Online Dictionary, 2006). One well established groupware example is Lotus Workplace which is a set of online work collaboration products from IBM's Lotus division, and the workplace products consist of Workplace Messaging, Workplace Team Collaboration, Workplace Collaborative Learning and Workplace Web Content Management. Lotus Notes which was developed by the Lotus Development Corporation in 1989 and was acquired by IBM since 1995, was one of the first applications to support users in accessing a distributed database of documents via a LAN or WAN. Furthermore, for many years, Notes was the main full-featured groupware solution. The Lotus team was encouraged to get new ideas to innovate, and with the work done, the innovative pieces were being folded back into the core brands (David, 2007). Lotus Workplace helps employees to communicate, share information and collaborate on various business tasks. Instead of dealing with a dozen separate applications, including instant messaging and email or paying for components that are rarely used, a mobile groupware application consolidates various applications into a single, integrated platform on one page. Users need not to log off and sign on to different applications to perform different tasks. A mobile groupware application enables users to participate in an online learning course or publish a memo for their company's intranet (a portal-based internal communication system in an organization). Additionally, it should provide instant, all time access to people and information, minimising the cycles associated with email and voicemail 'tag' and complex searches for timely information.

Mobile enterprise applications

Dissimilar to the mobile groupware application, the mobile enterprise application is pushed from the enterprise resource system which connects the enterprise database with mobile workers on any device and accelerate the working efficiency of the business process which contain multiple departments, such as Procurement, Production, Fulfilment and Financial Services, etc. For instance, as illustrated in Figure 4.2, the SAP Enterprise Portal was developed as a portal solution to SAP R/3 which integrated with the groupware system and groupware-related data (e.g. Lotus Notes/Domino). As a result, it not only works on the business process level, but features a groupware framework to increase transaction efficiency and productivity. Moreover, the portal application can be accessed through the Internet.

Enterprise mobility theory

Based on above research, we can conclude that an enterprise mobility application should provide the three following capabilities:

- **Web-based**: Which means mobile workers can grab needed information and collaborate with others through Internet;
- **Centralized Database**: All the involved data (e.g. transaction data, communication data) should be stored in a centralized database to reduce redundancy and easy management;
- **Integrated Applications**: The functions of the enterprise systems should be integrated together for easy access to increase usability.

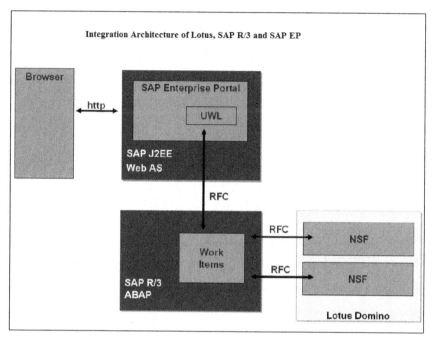

FIGURE 4.2 Integration architecture of Lotus, SAP R/3 and SAP EP
(adapted from SAP, 2005)

Further Ideation, one of the major areas of expertises in mobile enterprise application development, brings forward an enterprise mobility framework illustrated as Figure 4.3 which consists of two main components: Mobile App and Middleware.

Mobile Application is running in mobile devices and connects with middleware to provide a portal to the enterprise data. The application should work smoothly in different platforms and there are two approaches to realize the objectives: develop specific applications to the device platform or based on html/html 5 which makes enterprise databases serve as sites for easy access.

Middleware mainly includes the security mechanism and the access to enterprise data. The Authentication/Authorization layer aims to block the access of unauthorized users and to make sure the user gets the content according to the user's permission. The Business logic layer aims to attach specific services to the user, for example, Location Service allows the device to continuously update the location, Messaging Service uses the SMS Gateway to send messages, Business Process Service is in regard to conducting the business tasks, Payment Service allows payment requirements through the Payment Gateway and Analytics Service provides a mechanism for users to undertake relevant business analytics.

Based on the theory explained above, we can get an insight about how mobile application, Internet and enterprise database integrated together to realize enterprise mobility and provide connectivity. Moreover, as e-commerce increases, the demand for enterprise mobility is expected to grow which means the framework should allow flexible data sharing, access and collaboration.

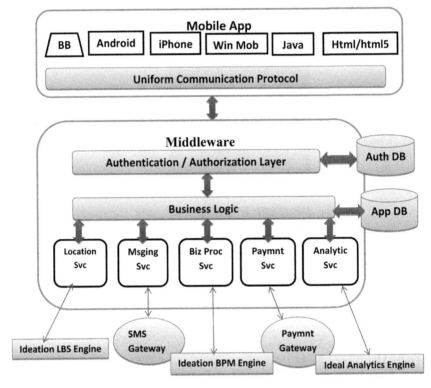

FIGURE 4.3 Enterprise mobility framework
(Adapted from: Ideation, 2011)

Enterprise Mobility Trend

"*Mobility + Cloud*" is not only changing the way people access enterprise and personal information, but also how mobile applications are developed, acquired and used within the enterprise, or utilized by the consumers (Endeavour, 2011). It can help to reduce cost, access/view/manage/share the content as soon as it is uploaded to the cloud storage, seamless data sharing, provide a secure enterprise data environment, simplify the process of using enterprise mobility and shorten the implementation cycle, and we can expect that the data will be stored in the cloud storage as well as in the enterprise application. As a result, mobile workers can directly operate the business through the cloud. According to IDC (2011c), the public cloud service market size was $21.5 billion in 2010 and is expected to reach a volume of $72.9 billion in 2015. In other words, the market is in an average annual growth rate of 27.6 per cent from 2010 to 2015. In addition, IDC estimates that public cloud computing expenditure will reach 46 per cent of the new growth in IT. Based on the research, IDC expects that cloud computing will be the main driving force of the IT industry in the next 25 years. No doubt, enterprise cloud-based computing will promote enterprise connectivity and provide a flexible choice to the enterprise.

Enterprise mobility development

According to BlackBerry (2008), before the enterprise goes mobile, it is important to figure out whether it is necessary to develop enterprise mobility and how mobile applications can fit into the business activities, and the following questions should be considered for the mobility plan:

- Is the activity which would be mobilized critical to the business?
- Does the business need real-time access?
- How will mobility benefit the enterprise: increase sales, reduce sales cycles, streamline workflow, improve business efficiency and productivity, reduce operational costs, improve data collection and accuracy or enhance customer satisfaction?
- Where will the mobile workers be when they access the information? Are the locations predictable?
- Will the workers have mobile devices and Wi-Fi access when required, even during transit?
- What kinds of tasks will be performed (e.g. respond to messages, invoice procedures, etc.)?

Once an enterprise determines to go mobile, it will have to make a "build" or "buy" decision. The consideration includes whether the IT department has the ability to develop the necessary application in-house, or is it more cost effective to outsource the application development, or will there be less expenditure in purchasing an existing mobile application?

Finally, to realize the enterprise mobility, there are three phases it will go through, namely discovery, development and deployment (BlackBerry, 2010).

- **Discovery Phase:** This phase mainly aims to gather the information that is required to develop an effective deployment plan. It consists of two main aspects: segment mobile users and identify which processes to mobilize. *Segment Mobile Users*: fully understand the mobile users to make the right mobility decision for the enterprise, which means to identify who will use the mobile application and their expectations (e.g. what devices, what processes, what applications, etc.). With the collected information, the mobile users can be categorized and this makes it easier to determine how to support them with mobility. *Identify Which Processes to Mobilize:* to decide which internal processes should be integrated (e.g. procurement, transaction, reporting, etc.). "Spending and resources should be focused on processes that provide the highest benefit and return on investment potential" (BlackBerry, 2010).
- **Development Phase:** The goal is to develop a workable strategy for going mobile which will be deployed in the following phase, and the plan should be flexible to further changes. BlackBerry (2010) agrees that the more time and effort taken during the Discovery Phase to segment mobile users and to review how enterprise mobility goals align with business objectives, the easier it will be to bring forward a suitable plan. Based on the analysis of the previous phase about

the mobile users and integrated business process, we can then investigate the key factors that need to be paid attention when developing the strategy:

- **Heterogeneous back-end integration:** The application should offer seamless integration with a variety of back-end data sources (e.g. database, web services, enterprise applications, etc.), which means the connection to all business critical data and processes should be guaranteed (Sybase, 2011).
- **Heterogeneous device support:** Multiple device types (e.g. iPhone, BlackBerry, laptops, tablets, etc.) should work smoothly with the application.
- **Business Functionality:** The application can fit into the business workflows and address specific tasks.
- **Security Protection:** The data security should be guaranteed from managing and limiting access to sensitive information assets, protecting against malware (e.g. virus, worms, Trojans and spyware), securing lost or stolen devices, safeguarding against Direct Attack (e.g. browser exploit, device interfaces), defending against Data Communication Interception (e.g. sniffing data when transmitted and received) and securing against Identify Theft (e.g. accessing resources with a user's identity) (AT&T, 2011).
- **Service Quality:** Minimizing user downtime with bandwidth optimization, which means all management tasks can be done regardless of bandwidth available, and provide a continuous plan to ensure the performance (Sybase, 2010).
- **Centralized Management:** Provide a single administrative console, so the manager can centrally manage, secure and deploy mobile data, mobile devices and the application.
- **Scale Extension:** The application should have the capability to support a growing number of users.
- **Usability:** The system interfaces should be rich and intuitive.

There are many mobile working applications available in the market to cater different needs and businesses should be careful when choosing one to make sure that it meets their requirements.
- **Deployment Phase:** In this phase, the mobility strategy will be executed, and its success depends on the time and effort that was spent in the Discovery Phase and Development Phase. Similarly, a well-designed mobility plan can help the organization decide which mobility projects to pursue in order to produce the best results (BlackBerry, 2010).

As the global economy develops, organizations need to work more dispersedly which will accelerate enterprise mobility. Enterprise mobility can help to increase business efficiency and productivity based on responses to requests in real time and improving data accuracy and usability. Regardless of industry or size, enterprise mobility is significant for business innovation, competitive growth and profitability.

In reference to a study by the University of Texas, the median Fortune 1000 business could realize a $2.01 billion annual revenue increase if they enhance the usability of the data by just 10 per cent (Sybase, 2011). The mobile era isn't the future, it's right now, and the wireless revolution is not just about to adapt mobile applications so the tasks can be done remotely, its ultimate goal is to adopt entirely new applications that will reshape the way we do business (BlackBerry, 2008).

Future of mobile technologies

The forecast of mobile technologies is that their growth will be even faster in the future and is estimated to expand and dwarf the desktop internet access by the year 2013. This forecast is based on the expected growth of five technologies and social trends namely; 3G and 4G, social networking, video communication, VoIP (explained below) and smart mobile devices. Many more people have Internet access via mobile phone than PCs. As shown in Figure 4.4, the growth rate in sales of mobile technology will continue to increase until at least 2015. The increased use of mobile technology is expected to drastically affect a number of industries and impact their operations as well as strategic management. Moreover, along with the development of mobile technologies, the demand for desktops and laptops continues to grow slowly compared to the growth of smartphones and tablets. Figure 4.4 suggests the sales trends of smartphone, tablets and PCs forward to 2020, with smartphones reaching 2 billion by 2020 and tablets overtaking sales of PCs at around 2016/2017.

Voice over internet protocol (VoIP) is a way of making phone calls over the internet and is not yet widespread among mobile users. However many smart phones offer user-friendly interfaces with VoIP with cheaper tariffs which are helping to increase their use. There are many companies such as Skype or Vonage which offer VoIP.

Web browsing is increasing on mobile phones as it allows easy hand and anywhere access for what they can do on laptop or PC, etc., on a small mobile screen. Live sports, music and radio services on mobile phones are also increasing. Mostly, people use the Internet on mobiles to get access to social networks such as Facebook and Google Plus. A mobile phone camera offers a natural way of capturing objects in the mobile user's

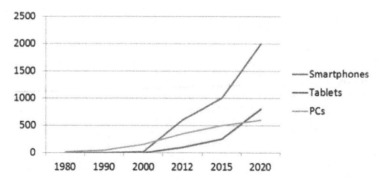

FIGURE 4.4 Smartphone, tablet, PC forecast to 2020
(Rules, 2012)

immediate surroundings. Users can circulate images straight away from different places. This could have a variety of uses for mobile working.

New broadband wireless technologies such as WLAN, Home-RF, UltraWide Band are coming out in the market and could coexist with or compete with 4G are emerging in the market. In Asia, several countries such as South Korea and Taiwan are aiming for a leading role in development of 4G and other related technologies. Mobile equipment can be built cheaply in Asia and this could also prompt other regions such as Europe and the US to invest in development, production and deployment of better mobile communication infrastructure.

Back-end systems

Mobile working can be very complex, especially with large businesses and the ICT systems supporting them. These back-end or so called core systems can be divided in several sub-categories and this section will cover some of the most common mobile-working-related systems.

Product applications

Most organizations have several different computer applications for their products. In some cases these systems were developed decades ago so they are often labelled 'Legacy Systems'. There are many problems associated with such systems including difficulties in integrating them with each other and with newer systems, inflexibility in terms of expansion or scaling down and rising costs of maintenance. These problems often result in hindrance to the implementation of mobile working.

Legacy systems often fall short in the provision of business information for compliance, sales and management needs or management decision making. This is mainly due to the fact that the data formats used are often incompatible with modern mobile working tools and without data from these core systems, the information would often be incomplete or misleading. These systems would have to be "hard-coded" even just to make a simple product or few changes, which can be very time-consuming and costly.

To improve customer service, the provision of information on timely bases, prevention of fraud and to support new agile business models, organizations need to deal with all the problematic issues associated with these legacy systems. One solution is, of course, replacement, but often high costs and unacceptable risks make this option unattractive. Another alternative is to reengineer these systems first and then wrap them with new technology, which can provide functionality as a service to other systems and allow changes to the core systems without the need to redevelop all systems. This approach, if executed well, can help link a company's infrastructure with modern business process driven applications. However, to implement it, organizations may at least have to partially implement the Service Oriented Architecture (described later in this chapter). In addition, very good project management and support from top management in terms of provision of required resources would be crucial.

Another solution is outsourcing, as there are third party companies and standard software packages available to manage mobile working. This option is often more risky and it is usually small or medium sized organizations that take it up because they may not have enough resources to build these systems themselves. To mitigate the risks, software packages and more importantly vendors have to be chosen carefully to ensure best fit with the existing organization. Future changes in the organization and systems architecture in particular must also be taken into account.

Whichever strategy is chosen, organizations need to ensure that new systems are business process and customer orientated rather than focusing on transaction orientation which is more common with traditional organizations and legacy systems. Integration with other systems which support different service delivery is also key to ensuring efficient enterprise-wide work flow information and providing a uniform look and feel. Security should always be a major priority when any changes in core systems are implemented. To this end, core systems may have to work with new biometric technologies, whether that takes the form of retinal scans, fingerprints or voice recognition. All these requirements and relevant solutions are demonstrated in the case study below.

Case study: Swindon Commercial Services (SCS) (Source: Consilium Technologies, 2008)

This case study was prepared by the author to facilitate class discussion rather than illustrate effective or ineffective management practices. Only publicly available material has been used to write this case and it does not reflect any opinions of employees or management at this organization.

Swindon Commercial Services (SCS) is part of Swindon Borough Council. It is responsible for providing traditional council services such as street cleaning, waste and recycling, highways maintenance, grounds maintenance, housing maintenance and support services, as well as work won through open tender, including construction and project work, catering, security and building cleaning. The organization has a turnover of £58m and employs 960 full-time staff. Within its Housing Maintenance division it manages the maintenance of over 11,000 properties.

Consilium Technologies, an IT company has provided SCS with a 100-user real-time system covering a range of mobile applications, branded TotalMobile, running on the Symbol MC9094 EDA and Microsoft Windows Mobile 5. These applications are integrated to their core back office systems such as Housing Management and CRM. The TotalMobile applications are built using the latest technologies from Microsoft including Microsoft SQL Server replication. Connectivity is provided by GPRS or Wi-Fi and the TotalMobile solution allows for times when users are out of signal range permitting them to continue working on with the job data resynchronising when back in coverage. The applications include:

- **Job Management** – Sends jobs and associated information to mobile operatives and allows them to update the back office with status and details of work completed in real time. This improves efficiency through enabling agile job scheduling.
- **Timesheets** – Provides detailed time recording either as a standalone solution or automatically via seamless integration with other TotalMobile applications.
- **Best Practice** – Assists in enforcing health and safety policies and duty of care for mobile workers.
- **Materials** – Manages Imprest van stocks allowing organizations to improve their management of stock based in mobile locations. This is integrated to back office systems in real time to provide constant stock replenishment.
- **Gas Appliance Servicing** – Captures regulatory appliance inspection and work information also ensuring records are updated and held centrally. Required documentation can also be produced on site.

SCS was challenged by Swindon Borough Council to transform itself into a successful commercial business providing a financial return to the Council. However, one of the major constraints to this change programme was thought to be the existing IT solution within SCS. A lack of investment had resulted in a weak technology platform that was unable to support the business in its quest for winning new work or retaining existing work in the short, medium or long term. Therefore, a key element in the transformation to a commercial operation was to improve the IT platform and undergo the associated business change. This would enable SCS to improve its overall service offerings, whilst at the same time generating organizational efficiencies and savings.

As part of the IT review, SCS was also keen to modernise its workforce and prepare it for the future. This centred on giving employees access to mobile working solutions in addition to an integrated job management system and modern call handling technology.

Improved IT capabilities and fast track implementation of new working practices. Better overall service performance, increased job completion rates, improved customer satisfaction, financial and service efficiencies as well as higher Council CPA and Housing ratings.

For SCS the business objective was to:

- provide a technology solution, which will equal and improve upon costs and services;
- meet the Authorities' corporate priorities;
- offer robust real time Management Information for SCS and its clients;
- enable real-time information to ensure jobs are completed at first point of contact;
- to enable SCS to compete on an equal standing with the market leader.

The application, which went live in just three months, is hosted in an offsite data centre and covers financials, repairs and maintenance of housing stock. TotalMobile is the application tier of an enterprise Windows Mobile strategy. It allows an organization to deliver and manage integrated mobile applications for field workers. TotalMobile is developed using Microsoft technology and provides a network diagnostic, casually connected applications platform. This means that TotalMobile applications continue to provide a seamless user experience regardless of network availability and that Total Mobile can use any available network such as GPRS, WiFi, etc.

Organizational Improvements Achieved Included:

- increase in job completion rate through 'right first time' leading to an increase in customer satisfaction;
- an 18.4 per cent productivity improvement on Housing Repairs contract, equal to 5 employees' work per annum;
- reduced travel and decision-making time resulted in efficiencies which equate to 5% of available labour per year;
- an increased efficiency of 10% in the back-office through process improvement;
- increased speed of job processing from call centre to site;
- saving in overheads of £30,000 per annum for multipart stationery.

What makes this solution particularly innovative, unique or otherwise significant is that all components of the solution are hosted in an off-site highly resilient datacentre. During heavy flooding this summer (2007) it proved itself invaluable as the customer's office was flooded and their systems would have been down for days had it not been hosted off-site. The mobile solution is built using Microsoft's latest development environment.net and utilises Microsoft's SQL Server Replication Services, allowing operatives and users to continue using the mobile solution even when out of range of any signal coverage. Housing repairs jobs are scheduled dynamically. As each user completes a job the system allocates the next most relevant task.

Middleware

Lack of integration with other systems is one of the most common reasons for the organizations not achieving desirable benefits from mobile working or other developments such as e-commerce. There are many ways of tackling the problem of integration, such as re-coding parts of existing systems or replacing them altogether, but one method, the use of middleware technologies, has been very popular and achieved widespread implementation by companies in a wide range of sectors. These technologies enable different types of systems to interact with each other and make it easier to integrate new systems which a company may implement in the future into existing infrastructure. There are many types of middleware technologies; Services Oriented Architecture (SOA) is the most popular. Potential benefits, such as reduced IT costs, systems integration and greater business agility have persuaded many organizations to adopt SOA (Knorr and Rist, 2005).

SOA is different from other computer applications development paradigms such as object oriented software development. The main advantages of SOA over other software development architecture is that by externalizing functionality into reusable components and organising them into a logical framework, it minimizes two of the greatest causes of delay – the need for exhaustive communication between the business and IT, and in most cases the need for IT to write code from scratch to develop new programmes or new functions for existing applications. In addition, organizations can also re-use their legacy systems as SOA enables legacy systems to communicate with other systems.

Chapter summary

This chapter was a presentation of various devices, networking solutions and computer applications available for mobile working. Clearly, there are numerous choices available to organizations and a decision to choose a right device, network or application is not easy. The selection process can be made easy by conducting a detailed analysis of mobile working requirements and matching them with available solutions. This is an iterative process and may take several cycles before a suitable solution is found which meets requirements as well as any budgetary limitations. The use of external consultants with the relevant experience might be helpful in aiding analysis to those organizations with no prior exposure to SOA.

5

USABILITY AND TRUST

Case study: Southern Water

This case study was prepared by the author to facilitate class discussion rather than illustrate effective or ineffective management practices. Only publicly available material has been used to write this case and it does not reflect any opinions of employees or management at this organization.

Southern Water provides the water supply and wastewater treatment services across Kent, East and West Sussex, Hampshire and the Isle of Wight. Southern Water has also embraced field force enablement. Its field workers across all areas of the business are linked to the central system via mobile phones with tiny, integrated keyboards. The system is well suited to coping with emergency work. All alarms are linked to the system. From the information on their screens they choose the best person to do the job. The normal week's tasks are planned in advance and sent to workers' mobiles each Monday (Case Source: DTI business guides).

Southern also has a graphical information system connected to mobile units in its vehicles which enables the company to know exactly where each worker is at any given moment. This means that in an emergency the nearest worker can be sent, the central system having checked that they have the requisite skills. Southern has worked to identify problems and communicate issues to staff, offering workshops to inform and train them. With a small device like the Nokia, there have been accidents where they are easily damaged. But they feel that the benefits outweigh the drawbacks. They have an overview of the whole business in one system which makes things easy and efficient (Stedman 2004).

Introduction

Due to the relative newness of mobile technologies, there are still a number of significant usability and trust issues which need to be addressed to achieve widespread adoption by employees. This chapter will provide detailed discussions around these themes and will offer practical advice on how to deal with this resistance to the use of, and lack of trust in, mobile technology.

User resistance to change

Mobile working systems and devices will be used by a number of different types of people including customers (in cases where mobile commerce is offered), workers in the field, executives, management staff as well as other interested parties such as trade partners. Many systems fail simply due to one or more types of user refusing to use a system or using stealth tactics to undermine the new system. This phenomenon is often referred to as user resistance. Resistance to change is implicit or explicit negative reactions against change, or restrictive forces opposed to any reorganization of work process and acquisition of new competences. To minimize user resistance, it is important to understand the main causes of user resistance. Generally speaking, user acceptance is often linked to two outcome variables: system quality and system acceptance. But underlying these are the more complex issues of cognitive and motivational factors which give rise to improved quality or improved acceptance.

The first step in dealing with user resistance is to ensure that users from all hierarchical levels are involved in consultations about the need for the new technologies. Consultations should include the choices an organization has and should continue throughout the development stage, including training and incentives for adopting new technologies or working practices. Ayadi (2006) argues that the failure of implementation of new technologies in organizations often occurs because the executives focus on financial and technical feasibility rather than organizational or social feasibility. An organizational or social feasibility study would have dealt with the core of user issues. It is also essential in mobile working to get mobile workers (arguably the most important users of the system) involved, but this is much more complex than the implementation of physically internal systems and requires different strategies. The involvement of mobile workers in feasibility studies, systems testing and so on requires a higher level of incentives than is required when the users are based in-house.

At implementation stage, some users may fear job losses, or loss of power or status (especially managers), which may result in a demoralized workforce. In extreme cases, some employees may even try to sabotage the new system in order to avoid the perceived negative consequences. This issue can be addressed by implementing a comprehensive human resources management strategy covering changes in working practices, job appraisal and training programmes.

The size of the organization is one of the key factors affecting the adoption of new technologies. The greater the size of the organization, the more resource and capital allocation is needed to facilitate adoption. The existence of a new technology's champions within top management also influences the adoption. Champions are needed amongst top management as well as at middle and lower ranks of an organization. Perceived usefulness is also widely believed to be a key facilitator of adoption. If people in an organization are convinced that a new initiative is good for the organization as well as for their own personal productivity and to ease work procedures, they become more motivated to adopt a new technology.

Many users will also be reluctant to adopt mobile working. Understanding the rationale in resisting mobile working is of value to companies in enabling the development of plans to achieve widespread adoption. What motivates someone to use mobile systems? Many would only use it if they perceive it to be providing higher value in terms of personal efficiency, better work-life balance and financial gains etc.

If lack of awareness is causing people to hesitate or resist mobile systems, organizations can launch a properly planned communications campaign to give information tailored to help in this situation. Organizations need to understand the nature of resistance in order to take this factor into account when developing a mobile channel. Organizatons should identify causes of resistance and address them directly. The feelings of insecurity and learning issues which are common barriers to adoption could be avoided by proper marketing campaigns, communication with mobile employees, training and user-friendly system design. To facilitate adoption, organizations also need to undertake a systematic approach to users' learning processes and adopt their tutorials and other training material in accordance to their unique learning needs.

Managing adoption

A number of factors contribute to success or failure of mobile working adoption within an organization. These factors include a company's commitment to mobile working, leadership of this initiative and involvement of stakeholders in the full process, from planning to actual implementation. Executives need to have a good understanding of the fast changing capabilities for related technologies and adjust their mobile systems' functionalities according to the business need and communicate the value of mobile working throughout the organization. Mobile working also requires systematic attention to organizational learning processes, organizational structure/ culture and technology infrastructure. A summary of critical success factors in the adoption of mobile working is given in Table 5.1. It presents a classification of success factors into three major categories: strategic, structural and management-oriented.

The factors in Table 5.1 suggest that, to realize the full benefits of mobile working, organizations need to develop a suitable vision for the firm, appoint a mobile working champion who owns the transformation process, create a collaborative organizational culture and implement a rigorous communication strategy to reduce resistance amongst employees and customers.

Within this new set of possibilities provided by mobile working, there are risks as well as opportunities for businesses and employees. However, owing to the security and trust issues discussed above, employee take up of mobile working has been much lower than expected. Many workers still lack the required IT skills necessary for mobile working. Unwillingness to adopt new working practices has also hindered progress in this regard. From an organizational point of view, failing successfully to adopt mobile working initiatives originates from a combination of unclear business vision for mobile working and a lack of technological expertise, among other factors. These other factors include: uncertainty of financial benefits, lack of time/resources to start new projects, high costs of computing technology, organizational issues like top management short-sightedness and longstanding internal barriers. These issues have been covered elsewhere in this book and will not be repeated in detail here.

Managing trust issues

Mobile technologies are fast evolving and competition between manufacturers and vendors is so fierce that some innovations are not fully tested and de-bugged prior to dissemination (Sohr, Mustafa and Nowak, 2011). They claim that there are very real risks for end-users and operators alike (and therefore susceptibility to fraud) due to technical insecurity and a large number of new mobile phones emerging into a largely unregulated market. They also claim that through the use of a Java-based Trojan horse it is possible for attackers to obtain manufacturer or even operator access permissions. These issues damage employee as well as management confidence in using these devices for security critical work. This lack of trust is a major hurdle in the growth of mobile working. Wang (2005) categorized trust in the following categories:

- *Trust and trustees:* The two parties, "truster" and trustee, are vital for establishing a relationship. In a mobile working environment, mobile working systems developers/vendors are trustees and businesses/employees are the truster.
- *Vulnerability*: Traditional businesses usually have a physical presence and employees work within those physical boundaries which reduce the sense of vulnerability but the anonymity associated with the mobile/online world leaves businesses and employees feeling more vulnerable. This is not just about vulnerability to fraud but also loss of privacy, because every move made by an employee can be recorded and analysed to assess their work behaviour. In some cases, this information may be used for promotion or disciplinary reasons, further fueling mistrust in most cases.
- *Produced actions*: An employee action may include just visiting the Intranet for information or to conduct other tasks such as ordering spare parts or stock checks, etc. Organizations will need to pay much more attention to security to win the confidence of their mobile employees as well as customers who would be concerned if their personal data was compromised during mobile working.
- *Subjective matter*: Trust is a psychological state of mind when the person is willing to accept the risks involved therefore it is a subjective issue. Some people will trust easily whereas others will not trust, no matter what. The majority of people, however, fall somewhere in between, and can be persuaded to trust. When the perception of the benefits outweighs the risks in the relationship, the person enters

TABLE 5.1 Summary of major success factors for e-mobile working adoption

Strategic factors	Structural factors	Management-oriented factors
Internet and related technologies used as a complement to the existing strategies	Right technological infrastructure	Organisation-wide commitment to mobile working, leadership (in terms of roles, responsibilities, budget matters and cross-functional interdependencies)
Basis of competition not shifted from traditional competitive advantages such as cost, profit, quality, service, and brand name	Good mobile working education and training to employees, management and customers	Support for mobile working from top management
New competitors and market shares tracked	Current systems expanded to cover the entire supply chain	Awareness and understanding of capabilities of technology by executives
Web specific marketing strategy	Good cost control	Communication of the mobile working value throughout the organisation by top management
Company's image and strategic position n the market strengthened		
Buyer behavior intelligence gathering and services personalization		
Good products and services offered		
Innovation facilitated		
Customer's and partner's expectations from the web well-managed		

into a trusting relationship (Carr, 2007). Therefore, the onus is on organizations to promote mobile working benefits and minimize the related risks (provision of institutional and structural safeguards) to facilitate trust.

The above characteristics show that trust is a complex issue needing careful consideration to understand what helps in establishing trust among trusters and trustees. These elements can be described as the integrity of a systems' vendor and their ability to deliver quality products/services while owning up to the consequences of a near future failure (guarantees). The element of integrity also includes an organization seen to be making all efforts to secure their systems. The presence of a clear privacy policy and its communication to all stakeholders inspires confidence.

Most people simply do not have the same confidence in their mobile devices as they do when using computers in their offices or homes. Although, as noted above, confidence might be increasing due to technological solutions such as the innovations in the development of more reliable and secure network connections, Paul Harris of UKFast urges consumers and businesses to be wary of complacency with regard to investment in infrastructures, warning that newly perceived "trust" in mobile device use is still fragile. He points out that the security fears of mobile devices and back-end/telecom infrastructure is very low on the agenda for most IT directors.

This warning is given because of the real risks being run by companies who are failing to invest sufficiently in the security of mobile infrastructure. It has been seen that security breaches and teething problems with devices can damage reputations, even for global giants such as Apple (in the case of iPhone 4). No company or technology, however successful or venerated, can be completely immune from failure.

The user interface is also considered to be of great significance in helping to build and maintain trust. As noted, a challenge mobile devices have faced are the small size of screens and keyboards on most of the devices in question. Companies have been driven to design, produce and implement new user interfaces for the consumer, all of which involve costly research and development. If the application turns out to be commercially unsuccessful then money and investment may be wasted. In order for users to be able to gain trust, companies have had to simplify their applications to give the users a higher quality experience of use. Rehman and Coughlan (2011) claim that the simplicity of the user interface, along with other factors, is vital if consumers are to feel confident in using the mobile technologies. Li (2010) highlights perceived ease of use and customization according to the users' preference as critical for winning users' trust.

Various methods such as digital signatures, encryption mechanisms and authorization functionality can relieve users' security concerns regarding mobile communication and enhance trust. In addition, clear policies and procedures for dealing with any security breaches also enhance the users' trust.

Human resources management

Human resources management is a key factor in the success of mobile working. Mobile working HR requires special skills because HR functions such as (HR) planning, job analysis and job design, recruitment and selection, job progression, appraisal process, training and compensation would be different in comparison to other traditional business models. Often, mobile working professionals, especially for internal mobile technologies infrastructure, need special skills and as a result they are still in short supply. The nature of mobile working operations also changes much quicker than other business functions so it brings a special set of challenges for HR as well as other managers. To succeed in this, managers must recognize the inherent differences between mobile businesses' operations and traditional fixed location businesses, and adapt to these changes.

The most obvious changes for human resources may include the need to identify employees with skills different from those found in more traditional organizations. People working in mobile working are often doing jobs that did not exist before and are working in an organization or division that did not exist before it in its current form. Therefore, basic human resource problems are exaggerated for mobile working. For a typical mobile working project, HR needs to recruit employees with a wide range of skills, such as:

- Technical staff like Web architects and designers experienced in creating mobile interfaces, mobile infrastructure specialists, Web developers, Website managers, security experts and team administrators.

- Business-focused staff like content experts.
- IT-related staff such as programmers and analysts.
- Managerial staff for strategic planning, relationship management, project management, content creation/management and process integration, etc.
- Managerial staff who are comfortable with line managing staff they may hardly see and also managing operations with the added complexity of mobile working.

In addition to these specific skills, knowledge, aptitude and other characteristics are desirable and should be combined in a proper way so they can work together to accomplish the desired goals. Since staff who are able to work on a mobile basis are often in short supply, skills that are in short supply must be used most efficiently. For example, some non-IT tasks (such as report writing, routine coding and systems administration) can be shifted to non-IT staff so that the IT staff can have more time to use their skills efficiently. A good understanding of these job roles, skills and issues would be required to recruit, retain, organize and develop mobile working departments or teams.

Another reason for a change in HR functions is that mobile working expertise is rare and employees with relevant skills are aware that they easily can find an attractive job in an active job market where their skills are highly valued. Problems in HR could mean that organizations lose these valuable employees. Some firms find that the changes resulting from mobile working can be best managed by a new organizational design. Some choose to create a separate division that handles the mobile working operations. This separate entity is usually expected to be integrated onto the rest of the operation after some time. These separate entities often have a more entrepreneurial culture which is suitable for mobile business operations so they are better able than their parent companies to attract the type of talent needed.

HR managers can experience a gap between understanding mobile-technologies based business operations and actually adapting their function to make the most of new opportunities. Understanding the capability offered by mobile technologies and designing an HR system to deliver optimal HR services may not be as easy as it sounds. Just like other changes, this change will also need to be carefully managed. For example, certain HR professionals (especially those who entered the field many years ago) traditionally are not as technology oriented as professionals in areas such as finance or operations and need considerable efforts in terms of training to adapt to this change.

To do well in managing human resources for mobile working, HR needs to build new organizational capabilities, rather than focusing on existing structures or hierarchies. These new capabilities may include flexible corporate DNA and culture, shared mind set and identification of key success factors or processes with a view to giving them priority. These capabilities are necessary whether mobile working is a small part of the business or constitutes a whole business.

Greengard (2000) suggested seven guidelines for HR managers who want to move at the speed necessary for managing human resources for online businesses. These guidelines are also applicable to mobile working.

1. Understand the fact that the online business is very different from other types of business. It requires learning new ways to communicate, creative thinking and less bureaucracy. The Internet creates new business opportunities but potential benefits can only be achieved if people are ready to move quickly and effectively utilize them.
2. Obtain the support of senior management. To do it, HR managers will have to justify the need for specific changes and clearly communicate the possible benefits of these changes.
3. Successful mobile working is multi-disciplinary and relies on participation from different departments, so a multi-disciplinary HR team also reflects the range of expertise and business knowledge. Team members must be able to communicate effectively and understand the differences in requirements of other team members. For example, an operations manager should have a good idea of technical issues involved and vice versa to be able to contribute positively. Decisions must be made quickly and put into actions swiftly.
4. Use different Return-On-Investment (ROI) calculations rather than traditional ones. Many initiatives in mobile working are new so it is difficult to measure the ROI objectively. Potential long term benefits should be taken into account along with hard financial figures.
5. Work with all departments within an organization to make good business decisions. Working closely with these departments will enable HR to collect information to see the effect of various decisions on the whole organization and not only in HR or mobile working.
6. Create an IT system that is flexible and scalable so that it supports the operations at a more efficient pace.
7. Do not let fear of mistakes or failure slow decisions and actions, the best systems may result in many mistakes being made (especially at early stages). Organizations should expect that the increased desire for speed will result in some mistakes and develop some tolerance to accommodate it HR functions should continuously analyse itself and organizational conditions and make any necessary changes as and when required.

For mobile working, strategies to achieve a competitive advantage need to view HR as a key function in implementing some of the relevant plans suggested above, to do well is a key cornerstone of success in mobile working.

Start-up costs

It appears that mobile operations are relatively easy to set up in comparison to those that are traditional physical-presence based. But on the other hand, start-up costs are high due to the purchase of expensive technology, back end integration costs and other costs associated with change management. However, it has to be done as an organization's strength and performance very much depends on its ability and capacity to implement efficient operations and for many organizations, mobile technologies will soon become a 'must have' capability rather than an option.

Chapter summary

This chapter covered a number of challenges and issues faced by managers when implementing mobile working. Consumer issues were discussed as well as employee management and some aspects of project management.

Trust is important to a firm's mobile working initiative. Although trust in mobile working shares many common elements with other technology-related trust, it is different in mobile working in that the technology as well as the organizational entity is an object of trust. The consequences of a breach in trust include loss of stakeholder satisfaction as well as failures in business operations.

To facilitate trust and enable change management, the human resources department can play a key role. However, it must be given the required resources and skills to support mobile-working-related HR issues such as creating accountability structures for the mobile workforce and recruiting the right people who can operate in a mobile working environment, etc.

6

SECURITY AND CONTINGENCY PLANNING

Case study: Staffordshire Police

This case study was prepared by the author to facilitate class discussion rather than illustrate effective or ineffective management practices. Only publicly available material has been used to write this case and it does not reflect any opinions of employees or management at this organization.

Staffordshire Police has 570 officers covering an area of 1,048 square miles with a population of over 1 million residents. The region includes rural communities, the large urban area of Stoke-on-Trent and numerous smaller towns and villages (*Computer Weekly*, 6 June 2005).

Staffordshire Police needed to increase the amount of time its officers spend on the street fighting crime. In the past police officers had to return regularly to the police station to report details of crimes and look up information on the Police National Computer Schrott (PNC) to assist in their enquiries. Information can also be passed on via the private mobile radio system. However, this requires dedicated staff in the police stations to look through the information on the PNC and pass this on to the officers, potentially causing delays.

Staffordshire Police approached a group of technology companies to provide a solution that would enable its officers to access information while on the beat. Officers can now securely access the PNC and crime reporting applications, via rugged PDAs. These PDAs use thin client technology to access servers running the PNC and crime reporting applications. Data is sent using the GPRS network enabling officers to send and receive information within seconds. No data is held on the devices, so without proper security codes, data cannot be accessed should any of the devices go missing.

Staffordshire Police will be using a secure leased line on the GPRS network. With an enhanced GPRS network across the county to ensure a high quality of coverage. According to Ian De Soyza, Project Manager, Staffordshire Police,

> The initial aim of enabling police officers to access mobile data was to increase the visibility of police officers in the community by 10 per cent. We have achieved this and are now working to further reduce the need for an officer to return to his or her station to carry out administration and reporting.
>
> The focus of the project was to ensure that the mobile access for the police officers was secure, stable and simple. Police officers can now access information from their mobile devices which has led to:

- Improved police visibility: Mobile access to the PNC and police reporting applications means that police officers can spend 10 per cent more time on the street as they no longer need to return to the police station to file reports.
- Faster access to information: Enquiries over the GPRS network take seconds to return detailed information directly to police officer at the incident site. This process used to be done over the radio, requiring an officer within the police station to look up the information and verbally pass on the information.
- Improved productivity: Police no longer need to return to the Police Station or Police car to make reports and access information, allowing them to spend more time liaising with members of the public and dealing with crimes.

Staffordshire Police are now looking at further developing the number and type of applications police officers can access from their mobile devices. This should enable the officers to spend even more time out of the police station.

Introduction

There are many security issues associated with mobile technologies, owing particularly to the wireless and open nature of these systems. Security is a key legal requirement and businesses must do their utmost to protect their valuable information. Reliability of the systems is also important as mobile working relies heavily on systems and any failure can be very costly. Businesses also need to plan for critical events and other system failures. This chapter will provide guidelines on how to manage security issues and how to develop robust plans to deal with any potential system failures.

Key security issues

Security-related issues are a major source of concern for the future of mobile working. Mobile devices increase security risks, potentially exposing traditionally isolated systems to the open and risky world of the Internet. Security problems can mainly be categorized as: hacking with criminal intent (e.g. fraud); hacking by 'casual hackers' (e.g. defacement of web sites or 'denial of service' – causing web sites to slow or crash); and flaws in systems providing opportunities for security breaches (e.g. a user is able to undergo transactions on other users' accounts). These threats have potentially serious financial, legal and reputational risks associated with them.

Information is a valuable asset and to fully utilize it, there needs to be wide availability, at least within an organization. However, security requirements might hinder wider information sharing. Therefore, organizational objectives of security and availability may be seen to pull against each other: the more confidential a set of information, the less available it would be. This has raised the question of 'available to whom?', and has led to a consideration of information as a human issue, as well as a technological and managerial issue. Drake and Clarke (2001) suggested a human-centred approach called a 'critically normative approach to information security' (Table 6.1). They propose a very different approach to information security to the one generally favoured.

The 'current view' may be seen as a set of guidelines or principles on which present approaches to information security are explicitly or implicitly based. The 'critically normative approach' provides the foundation for moving ahead to develop, pilot and refine an implementation framework for information security based on human issues.

Mobile security

To develop a mobile security plan, first, it is essential to find out the types of different threats and the security situation to get an insight into the development of security status. Second, it is important to find out mobile customer awareness toward mobile security. Based on which we can then develop the mobile security strategy and perform continuity planning.

Types of security threat

There are various types of threat that mobile users need to deal with currently and Figure 6.1 indicates the main purpose of designing the threats. The threat of computer viruses designed to invade privacy and, especially, steal money have increased significantly in recent years.

On the whole, most of the threats shown in Figure 6.1 are realized by mobile malware. The Intel subsidiary company – McAfee which is an antivirus technology security firm, released a mobile threats report on the third quarter of 2011. The research data is based on the study of 70 to 75 million unique samples. Figure 6.2 shows the malware growth in the entire mobile market based on the first three quarters from 2009 to 2011. Mobile malware growth has consistently risen since 2009, and McAfee described 2011 as the 'busiest year in mobile malware's history'. Furthermore, one of the most prevalent types of mobile malware is premium-rate SMS-sending Trojans to steal money and invade personal information.

In a mobile technologies environment, security threats largely come from the following:

- **Login detail disclosure:** This is the most basic threat to the mobile system. Using a number of means, criminals acquire login details, such as a username and pin, and use it to access the account to steal money from it. This threat could be mitigated through promotion of good practice amongst consumers to keep their login details safe and harder to guess.
- **Computer spy viruses:** These are computer programmes which are circulated through email or other means. Once a customer opens a malicious email, a programme is automatically installed in his/her mobile device. These programmes collect a login I.D. or other financial information which is used to conduct a range of criminal activity such as credit card cloning or unauthorized funds transfer.
- **Dummy sites or phishing:** Here, users are lured to a dummy or lookalike website. These websites look very similar to a genuine website, and when login details are entered, they are recorded and used for criminal activities.
- **Eavesdropping:** The attacker intercepts the conversation between a mobile phone (the user) and the base station (the caller). Generally, this is realized by installed malware in the user's phone which contains a means to capture the voice and record the conversation silently. This process can take place in the background and remain undetected. As a result, it would be difficult for users to notice that the conversation has been listened in to, and only sophisticated monitoring of the entire operating system or the generated communication data can detect the activities (Becher et al., 2011).

TABLE 6.1 An alternative future for information security (adapted from Drake and Clarke, 2001)

General View	Critically Normative Approach
Confidentiality / Restriction	Availability / De-restriction / Sharing
Information Restriction	Information Sharing
Pragmatic	Theoretical / Empirical
Technological / Computer Systems	Human Activity Systems
Instrumental	'Practical'
	Critically Normative. Apply Critique to:
	Normative Content
	Norms
	Boundary Judgements
	'System'
Pseudo-Scientific	Social
Rule-Based	Challenge the Rules
Truth	Normative Validity
Formal-Logical: Unreflective	Dialectical: Free to Think
'Is'	'Ought'
Functional	Radical
Accept the 'Material Conditions'	Critique of 'Material Conditions'
Rational equals Seeking the 'Truth'	Rational equals a dialectic between the 'involved and affected', all of whom are free to contribute

- **Availability attacks:** The goal of these attacks is to block the signal from the mobile phone or the base station, and therefore interfere with the legitimate communication of the user. For example, the attack can be realized via a jamming approach which will prevent the user from accessing the communication channel for a long duration of time.
- **Energy attacks:** An attacker can easily send wireless traffic to a victim node which requires the mobile node to process the traffic, but latterly realizing such traffic has no local relevance. As a result, additional power consumption is required to process the decoding, which slowly drains the battery of the device (Banerjee, 2007). Additionally, there is no explicit way for users to pre-filter such irrelevant traffic, so such simple attacks can effectively exhaust the battery of the mobile node and disrupt communication.
- **Location privacy attacks:** An attacker can detect the location of a user based on the monitoring of communication in the medium. For example, Banerjee (2007) states the attacker can triangulate the location of a transmitter based on the received signal strength, angle on arrival and similar properties.
- **Wireless devices attacks:** The development of wireless devices (e.g. Bluetooth, Wi-Fi) has brought along significant convenience to data transmission for users. Bluetooth enables users to communicate with each other directly, such as the ability to share personal data between mobile devices. But on the other hand, Bluetooth devices can broadcast presence and allow active connections and even transmission from unknown devices if the user does not configure the Bluetooth properly, which may result in the infection of malware. Wi-Fi provides the convenient connection between mobile phones and Wi-Fi hotspots, but if the user does not have a security mechanism to protect the data transmission, the fundamental vulnerability will provide lots of opportunities for hackers to intervene in the communication.

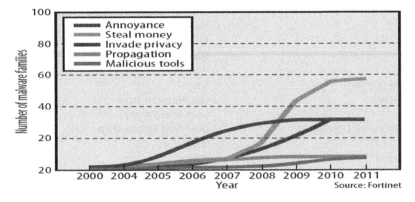

FIGURE 6.1 Purpose of mobile threat
(Lesvitt, 2011)

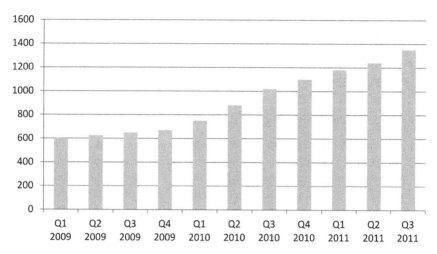

FIGURE 6.2 Total mobile malware growth
(Adapted from: McAfee, 2011)

- **Impersonation attacks:** In such attacks, the attacker's mobile phone can impersonate the device of the victim, and then use the service of a base station in a fraudulent way which may generate costs for the user and benefit the attacker.
- **Spam:** Mobile users may receive unwanted text messages, email and voice messages from advertisers which cause inconvenience for users to remove them. Moreover, in some cases mobile spam is used for fraudulent purposes, such as tempting users to send text messages or call chargeable service numbers. Also, mobile spam can be used for phishing purposes to lure users to type in passwords, private information or financial data via text message, email or web pages.
- **Mobile Botnets:** The number of victims that suffer from such attacks has been increasing in recent years. The most significant character of such attacks is that multiple mobile devices are under the control of the Botnet operator. Generally, the operator infects multiple devices with malware via email attachments, malicious applications or websites, and the malware includes command logic that gives the attacker complete access to the restricted data or remote control to the 'zombie' devices. As a result, the attacker can instruct to perform harmful acts which may cause loss to the user but benefit the attacker. The most frightening thing about this particular threat is that it is controlled by a central server (Sarah, 2009), which means the attacker has the ability to perform a more dominating control of the attacked phones, for instance, carrying out a particular task on multiple phones at a particular time, or perform a routing action at the same time every day, etc. Further, Table 6.2 provides an example of mobile Botnets and the affected devices:

The mobile network can open up a completely new world of opportunities and extend access to information well beyond the traditional confines of a PC to a power outlet and an Ethernet connection. Therefore, an unprotected mobile network can also open up sensitive private information to undesirable access. Moreover, there are an increasing number of users joining in with mobile networks and conducting tasks such as payments, transactions and social networking. In order to prevent this confidential information being attacked, it is important to design relevant strategies to improve the security status of the mobile communication network.

How does mobile malware get distributed?

Figure 6.3 indicates the share of mobile malware by platform by the third quarter of 2011, and it is obvious that Symbian malware dominates this section. But since the first quarter of 2011, the Android mobile platform has become the most "popular" platform for new malware which jumped around 35 per cent in the second quarter and 38 per cent in the third quarter. And based on the research results, McAfee states that Android is the principal target of today's mobile malware authors. Nevertheless, Chris DiBona, who is the open source and public sector engineering manager for Google, says that the threat of serious viruses spreading between Android devices is overblown and he argues that virus companies are playing on the users' fears to try to sell protection software for Android, RIM and IOS (Chris, 2011).

According to the research of PandaLabs which is an anti-malware laboratory, Trojans always act as the dominant malware category. Figure 6.5 shows the malware statistics of the third quarter in 2011 based on the capture of more than 5,000,000 new malwares, and it is important to notice that nearly three out of every four new malwares are Trojans.

Security awareness of mobile customers

To protect the users from the attack of malware, the installation of protective software is an important approach. But unfortunately, most mobile users have not been aware of this kind of protection. In reference to a mobile security report by McAfee shown in Figure 6.6, 79 per cent of users do not use any mobile protection software at all, and in addition, 15 percent of users are unsure whether there is any security software on their mobile devices.

The captured data above may not be fully accurate, but it provides an overview of the security status of the current mobile network. The threats generated by malware towards stealing money and invading privacy have increased significantly during the last few years and currently, Trojans are the primary malware tool. All major mobile platform users face mobile security issues, but most of them do not have a reliable mechanism to protect themselves from being attacked. Users of Symbian platforms are the foremost targets currently, but with the rapid market growth of Android and IOS, more and more attackers will focus on new targets.

Future mobile security trend

Along with more and more users joining the mobile network, and usage being focused on payment, transaction and social network, the threats designed to steal money and invade

TABLE 6.2 Mobile botnets

Mobile botnets	Affected devices
iPhone SMS	iPhone and iPad
DreamDroid	Google Android
ZeuS variant (Zitmo)	Blackberry
CommWarrior and Sexy Space	Symbian

privacy will increase significantly, and different regions face distinct levels of security. Lookout, which is a smartphone security company, released the 2011 Mobile Threat Report that was based on the aggregated data from more than 700,000 apps and 10 million devices worldwide (Kevin, 2011). Based on the research, the organization predicts the likelihood of encountering malware worldwide and the result varies from less than 1 per cent to more than 4 per cent depending on country as Figure 6.7 shows.

From Figure 6.7 we can conclude that the mobile security distribution can be observed based on developing countries and developed countries.

- The developing countries (e.g. China, India, Russia, etc.) which currently have rapid economic growth and high population density, are more likely to be attacked. Subsequently, we can assume that along with the economic development, there will be more applications like mobile banking and email in developing countries compared to developed countries. But on the other hand, policy governance related to mobile devices is weaker than developed countries. Therefore, these regions are more likely to be targeted. Additionally, Southeast Asia has a huge market base of Symbian platforms which is the main target of

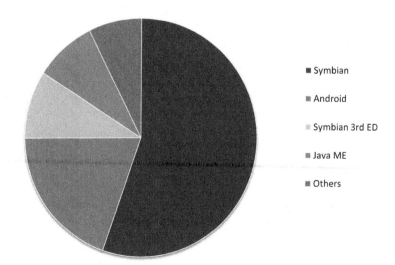

FIGURE 6.3 Total mobile malware by platform
(Adapted from: McAfee, 2011)

malware currently. Compared to developing countries which have a significant potential for economic growth, the developing countries that have an under-developed economy (e.g. South Africa, South America, etc.) are less likely to be targeted.

- Developed countries (e.g. Europe, North America, Australia, Korea and Japan) have a high availability of Internet and as a result, the mobile applications for banking and email may not be as diversified compared to those in developing countries. Furthermore, these countries have a relatively highly regulated mobile communication market which leads to a safer mobile communication environment. However, along with the diversity of mobile applications from third

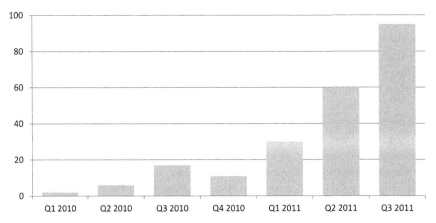

FIGURE 6.4 Android malware by quarter
(Adapted from: McAfee, 2011)

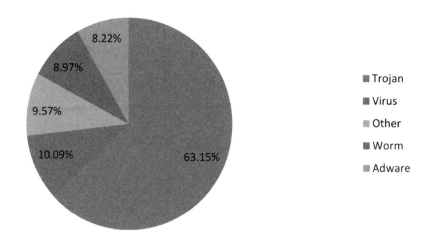

FIGURE 6.5 Malware statistic
(Adapted from: PandaLabs, 2011)

parties and the development of smartphones, mobile security issues will also be rising.

Mobile security strategy development

Along with the rise of mobile networks, concerns about mobile security have also been growing. It is important to design a comprehensive security strategy to protect the mobile device from attacks. Here, two aspects are discussed, namely the mobile security criterion and mobile security strategy development.

Mobile security criteria

To judge whether the mobile data is secure, three fundamental objectives are required to be considered: confidentiality, integrity and availability. Refer to Federal Information Security Management Act (FISMA):

- Confidentiality: "Preserving authorized restrictions on access and disclosure, including means for protecting privacy and proprietary information" [44 U.S.C., Sec. 3542]. A loss of confidentiality happens when the information is disclosed (e.g. read or copied) without authorization.
- Integrity: "Guarding against improper information modification or destruction, and includes ensuring information nonrepudiation and authenticity" [44 U.S.C., Sec. 3542]. A loss of integrity happens when the information is doctored or destroyed (e.g. modified or erased) without authorization.

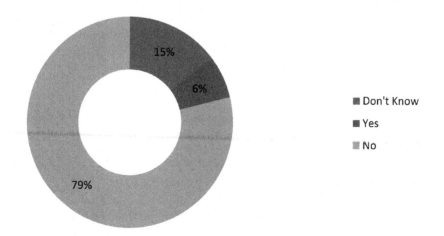

FIGURE 6.6 Use of mobile protection software
(Adapted from: McAfee, 2008)

FIGURE 6.7 Malware distribute statistic
(Adapted from: PandaLabs, 2011)

- Availability: "Ensuring timely and reliable access to and use of information" [44 U.S.C., SEC. 3542]. A loss of availability happens when the access to, or use of, information is disrupted.

The three fundamental elements mentioned above should also be ensured based on two aspects: a mobile platform system and mobile data transmission. In a mobile platform system, the application software has no privilege to perform harmful actions to other applications or the system or user's private data, such as read/modify user's data or read/modify the file of another application, etc. Mobile data transmission refers to data exchange between a user's mobile device and base station or data transmission between different users through Bluetooth or Wi-Fi. Thus, a sound mobile security strategy should provide the mechanism to protect the data confidentiality, integrity and availability based on the mobile platform itself and the data transmission.

Mobile security strategy

Many technical as well as managerial types of solution are available and each show various degrees of success. One of the main problems with implementing security solutions is users' resentment against several layers of security which might lead to less use. Another problem is the high cost associated with them; most sophisticated systems can only be implemented with the highest value parts of mobile systems. Hackers are not the only security threat, employees or contractors can do as much damage as a hacker can. Therefore security provisions are also necessary for internal threats.

In the face of multi-faceted, multi-directional security threats, implementing ad hoc security systems may not be the best approach. McDougall (2007) suggests that organizations need, as a minimum, to have:

- a strategic approach to security, building best practice security initiatives into systems and networks as they are developed;
- a proactive approach to security, involving active testing of security systems, controls (e.g. penetration testing), planning responses to new threats and vulnerabilities and regular reviews of internal, as well as external, threats. Advice from financial regulators can be sought on how to do it;
- sufficient staff with security expertise and responsibilities;
- regular use of system-based security and monitoring tools. This may include the use of digital signatures (a security option that uses two keys, one public and one private, which are used to encrypt messages before transmission and to decrypt them on receipt), or Public Key Infrastructure (policies, processes and technologies used to verify, enrol and certify users of a security application. A PKI uses public key cryptography and key certification practices to secure communications), etc.
- continuity plans to deal with the aftermath of any security breaches.

It is impossible to have completely fool-proof systems and security breaches are always a possibility so organizations must have processes in place to deal with them. It is important to provide clear and simple guidelines to consumers about what to do when they fall victim to fraud. In a mobile environment, consumers need to consider the following aspects to keep the mobile data secure:

- **Regularly backup:** Mobile users should backup the mobile information to computers regularly to help restore lost or damaged data when a mobile device has been lost or attacked by hackers.
- **Regularly update:** The mobile system and applications may consist of security weaknesses which could be made use of by attackers. To avoid such an attack, it is important for mobile users to update the system and the application software regularly.
- **Avoid sensitive information:** Sensitive information (e.g. password, credit card, personal identifiable information, etc.) should be stored on a separate device instead of mobile devices.
- **Use of protection software:** This is an important method in protecting the mobile device from the attack of hackers. The use of protection software (e.g. firewall or anti-virus) can significantly secure the mobile device from many negative aspects, for example, protecting the stored data and back transaction, detecting the danger before malware infects the system and stops the process, and it can provide the functionality of a telephone or SMS backlist, etc. The protection software can provide relatively comprehensive protection to a mobile device and it is easy for users to implement such a mechanism.
- **Use of Cloud technology:** Cloud technology has become a new trend in Internet usage. Cloud computing not only provides sound functionality to users, but also enhances the security of data. Cloud computing has a minimum requirement for the user's device and the basic requirement is a connection to the Internet. Furthermore, the Cloud server is managed by experts to ensure the storage centre is reliable and secure. As a result, users no longer need to worry

about data security if a mobile device is damaged or if data loss, implantation of malware or other problems occur.

- **Disable unused services:** Services such as Wireless, Bluetooth, Infrared or other connection devices should be disabled when they are not in use. Many users may leave these devices turned on for convenience even when the devices are not in use, but this behaviour is an invitation to hackers. Moreover, it is dangerous to connect to an unknown free Wi-Fi spot, as the hacker can capture transmitted data between the mobile device and the Wi-Fi spot easily. Disabling the unused transmit device is one of the most effective way to keep users from leaking privacy information.

- **Secure source:** Mobile users should visit authentic sources, websites and applications from a third-party, etc., and stay clear of downloading resources from insecure sources to avoid the rate of phishing and malware infection.

- **Strong password:** User IDs and passwords should be strengthened to reduce the rate at which they can be de-encrypted. This can be done when one sets up a connection (e.g. wireless or Bluetooth) or signs up to a new account, etc.

We are currently moving from the Internet society to a mobile society where more and more access to information is obtained through mobile devices (Becher et al., 2010). The more widely mobile technology is used, the more likely mobile users are to be the target of hackers. It has been an important issue to build a secure mobile network, and it can be realized based on two dimensions: mobile organizations and mobile users. It is also important to realize that building a secure mobile network is a bilateral responsibility for both mobile organizations and mobile users.

Continuity planning

Continuity planning definition

To ensure the mobile network provides a continuous service to mobile users, business continuity planning is required. Business continuity, which is the implementation of disaster recovery systems, is another fast developing area and is receiving much more attention now due to ever increasing risks from natural disasters and terrorism. In the US, for example, many organizations were directly affected by the destruction wrought by Hurricane Katrina in 2005. They learnt the hard way how unprepared they really were. The damage was so severe in certain regions that some organizations couldn't bring up applications until six months after the hurricane (Amato-McCoy, 2006). Costs of unplanned or even planned downtime can spiral as most mobile banking systems need to be available all the time. So it is essential for companies to undertake business continuity plans to effectively manage the risks around them.

Business continuity planning (BCP):

> identifies [an] organization's exposure to internal and external threats and synthesized hard and soft assets to provide effective prevention and recovery for

the organization, whilst maintaining competitive adventure and value system integrity.

(Elliot et al., 1999)

In addition, continuity plans need to be revisited and updated every three months as a minimum, as one or more components of the continuity system may not work when needed. Regular testing, simulation of disasters and mock recovery exercises are often needed to uncover any weak links. Every scenario and every possibility needs to be accounted for, drills need to be exercised and recovery plans need to be put into action. This will ensure that organizations can get back to business quickly in the event of a disaster. Furthermore, in reference to the research of Overland Storage (2010), the primary causes of business continuity/disaster recovery are:

- Hardware 44 per cent: A system component fails (e.g. servers, switches, disk or another core piece of infrastructure) causing a failure to meet service requirements.
- Human error 32 per cent: The primary cause of human error is either a mistake in a configuration setting or executing a wrong command in the system.
- Software and firmware error 14 per cent: Generally, these problems are related to operating systems hanging, driver incompatibilities and the introduction of new applications to servers.
- Virus/security breach 7 per cent: IT devices face high threats from malicious attacks. The company data stored in the server or the customer data transmitted between a mobile device and base station can easily be the target of hackers.
- Natural disaster 3 per cent: It represents a relatively small percentage compared to other causes, but these disasters are often cited as a leading reason for business discontinuity and this is the most significant aspect which requires to be considered when setting a continuity plan for a mobile infrastructure.

Development of continuity planning

Based on the business continuity research of AT&T (2011), the continuity plan for mobile infrastructure can be conducted based on six key steps:

- Step 1: Identify critical business processes and impacts
  The first step is to understand fully the critical functions of each part of the mobile infrastructure, the vulnerable areas in the structure (e.g. fires, floods, out of power) and how different disaster scenarios can impact the continuity of operations. The key is to identify critical processes and the time periods for when these processes are required (Storkey, 2011). This can help determine the resource usage from customers in terms of the time period (e.g. minutes, hours or days) based on discrete locations.
- Step 2: Perform risk assessment, mitigation and management
  The risk assessment aims to ensure the appropriate investments are made based on time and money. The assessment will identify the functions, processes, resources, suppliers and the organization's ability to achieve its mission objectives. In

addition, the potential threats, existing vulnerabilities and the probability that the threat will exploit the identified vulnerabilities should be identified and assessed (AT&T, 2011). These processes can be realized by convening workshops and brainstorming sessions.

- Step 3: Determine recovery strategies
  Once the business analysis has been completed, the continuity strategies relating to addressing the specific threats towards the mobile infrastructure will be developed.
- Step 4: Develop business continuity/disaster recovery plans
  The result of the risk assessment and the relative recovery strategies will be used to conduct the continuity plans to address exposed threats and a business continuity planning report may be submitted to the senior managers for decision making. The report should identify the risks, required techniques for mitigation/management, the recommended actions to address the problems and an estimate of costs. A superior manager can then assess the cost-risk before making decisions and seeking approval (Storkey, 2011).
- Step 5: Test, train and exercise
  The business continuity plan should be put on standby for implementation at any moment. They must also be tested on a regular basis to make sure the continuity solution can work effectively when a disaster strikes. The staff who will perform the process need to understand their roles and responsibilities in compliance with the business continuity plan and this requires comparative training with exercises. Based on the international experience, we can conclude that no matter how well the business continuity plan is designed and thought-out, it will very rarely work in practice without realistic and robust testing (Storkey, 2011), so testing should be frequently undertaken (e.g. at least every three months) to ensure the dependability of the continuity plan.
- Step 6: Monitor and improve performance
  Based on the results of each test and the changes to the mobile infrastructure, the business continuity plan should be evolved as well. In other words, an improvement or update of the continuity plan should occur over time as experience is gained and particular focus should be directed at areas where there is a history of incidents or events.

Contingency planning benefits

Sound business continuity support can provide specific expertise and services that ensure a company's capability to maintain operations cost-effectively despite a crisis, and once the relative continuity plans are applied, the business continuity solution should present substantial benefits (Kristen and Trude, 2001).

- **Reduced downtime:** When there is damage caused by a disaster, there will be backup plans to temporarily recover the infrastructure to reduce downtime, and the efficient recovery plan can provide a reliable service support to users.
- **Increase weakness awareness:** Business continuity planning can help create awareness of current mobile infrastructure issues and improve it.

- **Enhance service reliability:** The continuity plan will make the mobile infrastructure more robust. It strengthens the capability of the organization not only to deal with large-scale problems, but also to counteract small problems that may cause interruption to the service provided to mobile device users.
- **Enhance customer loyalty:** The application of a sound business continuity plan shows that the organization can keep their commitments to users and indicates that the provision of quality service is a high priority for the organization. As a result of building a good reputation, users become more confident about the organization and are much more likely to stay loyal.
- **Reduce losses:** The business continuity plan will significantly reduce losses for the organization if hit by a disaster.

Contingency planning risks

- **Availability:** The continuity plan is usually only available for a limited period following a disaster and as a result, the business continuity plan may lie forgotten in a desk drawer and become increasingly impractical to use in a real emergency.
- **Over reliance on support:** As an industry completes the business continuity plan with the support of a third party, over reliance on the consultants may occur and result in the exposure of confidential organization strategies to the third-party when the company's staff interact with them. Consequently, there would be a risk of confidential information being leaked by the third party.

The aim of the continuity plan is to ensure the business functions will be available to mobile users who expect supplies and services to continue in all situations (e.g. power failures, natural disasters, human error, network failures or other issues). Although the cost is huge, taking a proactive approach to business continuity is essential for the organization to be fully prepared in response to a disaster when it strikes (AT&T, 2011). The activities of continuity planning aim at the provision of seamless customer service even during the disaster. In other words, the continuity plan should help to maintain customers' use of the services (e.g. communication or data transmit) immediately following the crisis and work until the recovery process is finished.

Chapter summary

Information Security management is another area covered in this chapter. Information security in mobile working is very much dominated by technologically biased, operationally focused pragmatic controls. Human considerations are largely ignored, so we have suggested an approach informed by social theory. The approach gains its credibility on an explicit basis in social theory, from which an evaluative model and method of implementation have been crafted.

7

MOBILE WORKING PROJECT MANAGEMENT

Case study: Bank B, US (Extracted from Avison and Torkzadeh, 2009)

This case study was prepared by the author to facilitate class discussion rather than illustrate effective or ineffective management practices. Only publicly available material has been used to write this case and it does not reflect any opinions of employees or management at this organization.

This case is a demonstration of the management of a project about a "receipt imaging system" implementation at a midsize credit union bank in the US. To protect the identity of the bank and individuals, we call it Bank B. Bank B has more than $350 million in assets and over 30,000 members. It has a number of branches and ATMs in the area it serves and through the Internet in the entire US.

During 2000–2001, they started implementing a receipt imaging system. The system enabled Bank B to capture certain parts of the receipt with customers' personal details and signature and store it in an easily searchable database. Before this system, the receipts were stored manually, making later searches a very difficult and costly task. The new system promised to make it very inexpensive and quick to refer to a particular transaction at any stage.

When the system was being considered by Bank B's top management, several vendors approached them with their particular solutions. After a lengthy consultation process with the bank, they chose to go ahead on the promised benefits of cost savings and efficiency. They chose the most cost-effective vendor with a good track record but no prior experience of dealing with the existing systems used by Bank B.

Bank B's CIO appointed an experienced technical manager to oversee the project because he considered this project to be primarily about software installation and user training. He was given whatever human/financial resources he needed. His initial task was to adopt a new type of Internet address (IP) for each of their work stations because their chosen system didn't work with a standard IP address, which proved to be quite expensive. About six weeks later, a system, adopted/modified from a previously developed system by the vendor, was ready for testing. At testing stage, a number of technical problems were encountered by the vendor's engineers, delaying the completion by several months. Before that work could be completed, a new version of the software came along which meant that testing had to be started from the beginning. The new version also had a number of technical problems resulting in low morale and hostility at Bank B towards the new system and the vendor.

Due to these technical as well as management problems, both Bank B and their vendor appointed a new implementation team which managed to succeed in ironing out the problems. This was done through clarifying roles and responsibilities, clear scheduling, clever resourcing and firm commitments from the top management of Both Bank B and the vendor. The system was implemented and proved to be a success soon after. Although the final outcome was very positive, the project which was due to be completed in three months, took several years and costs were well beyond the original budget. Bank B realised most of the promised benefits but return on investment was delayed by several years.

Introduction

Project management is an important concept in information systems development as well as implementation of most other business initiatives. Often, the development or implementation of information technology or managing change will be run as projects and managed using various well established project management techniques and tools. Information systems development and implementation is often treated like a large-scale project and broken into several small-scale projects to manage various different aspects (called project portfolios), ranging from business process changes to make the organization ready for new technologies to the actual implementation of technologies. This chapter is an overview of project management as a subject and its application in the area of mobile working project management. It will discuss reasons for treating mobile technology implementation as an organization wide project. It will also cover the most common methods of project management and technological tools, such as PRINCE2, which help manage projects.

Project management overview

Project management methodologies offer a systematic approach to all stages of a project by providing guidance on how to plan, monitor and measure every step in a project. Project management is defined by the Project Management Institute (PMI) as the application of knowledge, skills, tools and techniques to a broad range of activities in order to meet the objectives of a project. A project is temporary and its time frame may vary from a few days to several years, depending on the scope of the project.

Another related concept in this context is Programme Management. PMI defines Programme Management as the coordinated management of a portfolio of projects to achieve a related set of business objectives. In other words, programme management is about the coordination of several projects to maximize the efficient use of organizational resources and to interlink strategic objectives. A large mobile working project may have to be divided into many smaller independent projects in which case the practices employed in programme management would become helpful.

A project may involve a number of steps such as a feasibility study, determination of objectives, planning, resources allocation and execution as well as an end-of-project evaluation. A number of project management tools, such as MS Project or PRINCE2 (covered later in this chapter) are available to support these steps.

Traditional project management methodologies offer a structured, low risk and rigid approach to project management, but this approach may not be most appropriate in the implementation of new technologies, such as mobile working, which are often implemented in external, customer-facing environments. Project managers often have to be willing to take greater risks and use flexible and unorthodox approaches. This is mainly because mobile working projects are close to the core activity of the organization (promoting and selling their services) so they are likely to use an approach which leaves the highest number of options open and allows for quick adjustments to respond to the fast changing technologies, market place and customer preferences. For such projects, Avison and Torkzadeh (2009) recommend the following steps:

- Aligning the projects with organizational goals – this seems obvious but too many technology projects are driven by technical issues rather than a sound business case.
- Defining project scope.
- Select an appropriate project management methodology such as MS Project or PRINCE2 to help complete the tasks.
- Developing a detailed project plan – estimating project costs and benefits and assessing risks.
- Building a multi-disciplinary project team to ensure quality.
- Using an established IS development methodology (one example is life cycle given in Figure 7.1) if developing the system in-house or assessing the case for outsourcing.
- Measuring project success.
- Project closure.

These steps are not linear and can be used or re-iterated as and when necessary. In this chapter, we describe the traditional project management methods but with a flexible approach used in technology-related projects.

Project planning

Implementing mobile working is often a large-scale business initiative requiring large-scale financial investment as well as the availability of a pool of human resources with a range of specialist skills such as technological, marketing, change management and project management.

In the case of large-scale systems, a number of development, implementation and management activities (presented in Figure 7.1) become independent projects themselves, so an organization requires programme management as well rather than just project management. For example, the mobile working adoption process has to be carefully planned and executed and is often seen as a project in its own right. In most technical projects, time and budget constraints could prove to be serious problems, as would be the handling of any organizational transformation processes. To deal with these issues, support from top management is seen as a key ingredient for success of a project. It often needs a champion amongst top management (generally the board of directors). Lack of senior management support can lead to failures because without it, obtaining the required resources to bring about the necessary changes in an organization can prove impossible.

Setting success criteria

Project evaluation is essential in understanding and assessing the key aspects of a project that make it either a success or failure as this is often just a matter of perception. Assessment of a system project's outcome is important to most of those involved in development projects – whether as a developer, customer, manager or any other stakeholder – for different, and possibly conflicting reasons. For example, a developer may regard good functionality of a system as a success, whereas for a senior manager, the impacts of a project on organizational productivity may be the main measure of success. Thus, there is a clear need for some comprehensive success indicators to be agreed before the start of the project. Existing literature proposes a number of different frameworks for evaluation of success in technological projects which are discussed here.

The concept of system project success has been an intensely debated issue in management literature. Success means different things to different people. A software engineer may consider success in terms of software functionality, an engineer in terms of technical competence and a human resources manager in terms of employee satisfaction. A review of the project management literature does not provide any consistent interpretation of the term 'project successes'. Delivering within budget or allocated time are often seen as key success measures and for this reason, technology projects are often deemed failures upon completion because few are completed on time and within budget due to high complexity and unknown variables.

There are numerous problems associated with evaluating/assessing the effectiveness of technology projects. However, many researchers have proposed a number of models to measure project success. For example, DeLone and McLean (1992 and 2003) proposed a model for IS success in 1995 and later amended it to be used in e-commerce projects.

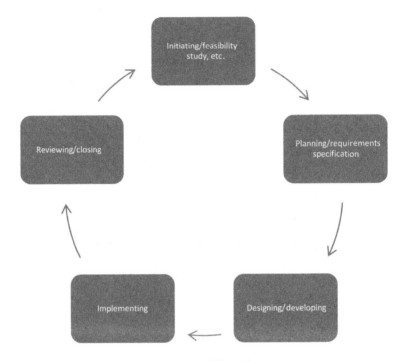

FIGURE 7.1 Information systems development life cycle

The DeLone and McLean (1992) model (see Figure 7.2) was an attempt to bring many success measures into one model and suggests an existence of interdependencies between its components. By studying the interactions among these components of the model, as well as the components themselves, a clearer picture should emerge as to what constitutes project success. They also proposed an update of their model in 2003 (See DeLone and McLean, 2003). The updated version of their framework is mainly specific to evaluating e-commerce information systems.

Seddon (1997) criticized this model and suggested that DeLone and McLean tried to do too much and as a result, it is both confusing and mis-specified. He proposed a revised model (see Figure 7.3). In his model, he replaced 'use' which he argued is a type of behaviour and not a success measure, with 'perceived usefulness' and added 'society' as a stakeholder, which he argues, is impacted by the success or failure of a system. Seddon's model also consists of several complicated relationships.

The feedback loop from perceptions (user satisfaction) back to expectations recognizes the importance of learning. The model asserts that expectations are continuously being revised in the light of new experiences with the system. In a clockwise fashion, revised expectations lead to revised perceptions of the project success and ultimately, back to revised expectations.

Shenhar et al. (2001) proposed a multidimensional framework for assessing project success which could be modified and used in mobile working projects. In this approach, projects are classified according to the technological uncertainty at the project initiation stage and their system scope, which is their location on a hier-archical ladder of systems and subsystems. The approach is presented in Table 7.1. It has 13 success measures, arranged into four dimensions: project efficiency, impact on customer, business success and preparing for the future.

The first dimension is concerned only with efficiency of the project management effort. This is a short-term dimension expressing the efficiency with which the pro-ject has been managed. It simply tells; how a project met its resource constraints, whether it finished on time and whether it was within the specified budget. The second dimension relates to the customer, addressing the importance placed on customer requirements and meeting their needs. The third dimension addresses the immediate and direct impact the project may have on the organization. It also relates to the following in a business context: did it provide sales, income and profits as expected, did it help increase business results and did it help gain market share? The last dimension is aimed at measuring long-term benefits from a project and it addresses the issue of preparing the organizational and technological infrastructure for the future.

Shenhar et al. (2001) suggests that:

- The first dimension can be assessed only in the very short term, during a project's execution and immediately after its completion.
- The second dimension can be assessed after a short time, when the project has been delivered to the customer and the customer is using it. Customer satisfaction can be assessed within a few months of the moment of purchase.
- The third dimension, direct success, can only be assessed following a significant level of sales being achieved, usually after one or two years.
- The fourth dimension can be assessed only after a longer period, probably two, three or even five years.

The application of this framework's different dimensions would vary from project to project and emphasis on different dimensions would also change. For example, in a complex project such as mobile working, the emphasis may be on meeting requirements rather than meeting the project schedule. In a relatively simple project, the emphasis may be on the efficiency dimension and a lower level of tolerance of cost or schedule overruns. Emphasis also changes according to technological uncertainty. For example,

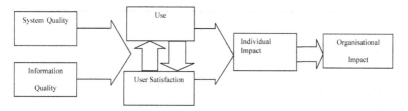

FIGURE 7.2 The DeLone and McLean model of information systems success (adapted from DeLone and McLean 1992)

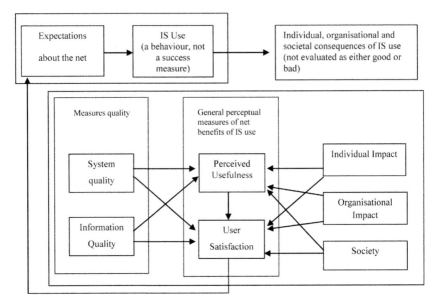

FIGURE 7.3 Seddon Model of IS Success: partial behavioural model of IS use (adapted from Seddon, 1997)

greater uncertainty may mean greater importance of future potential, whereas low uncertainty may mean greater importance placed on budget and schedule aspects.

Shenhar et al. (2001) proposed this approach with a premise that projects are part of the strategic activity of the organization and must be executed with an organization's short-term, as well as long-term, objectives in mind. They stress that project managers should act strategically, with their activities focused on business needs and on creating a competitive advantage with winning products. Thus, assessing project success would relate to both performance during execution and success of the end results. For this reason, unlike Baccarini (1999), they do not distinguish between project success and product success. Shenhar et al. (2002) also claims that this framework could be helpful, not only to all parties (project managers, teams and top management), but also throughout the entire life cycle of the project (selection, definition and execution).

It is important to remember that, even with a sophisticated success measurement framework, success will not be easy to measure. Baccarini (1999) recommends that the following factors should be considered when interpreting success.

- **Success has hard and soft dimensions.** Some project success criteria are objective, tangible and measurable (hard), such as budgets or schedules, and others, such as benefits to an organization or to society, are usually subjective and often difficult to quantify.
- **Success is perceived.** Different stakeholders may have their own particular subjective perception of success, depending on their needs and how well these

TABLE 7.1 Project success framework (adapted from Shenhar et al. 2001)

Success dimension	Success measures
Project Efficiency	Met project schedule
	Stayed on budget
Impacts on customer	Met functional performance
	Met technical specifications
	Addressed most customer needs
	Solved a customer's problem
	The product is used by customers effectively
	Customer satisfaction
Business success	Commercial success in terms of profit or growth
	Creating a large market share
Preparing for the future (Long term benefits)	Creating a new market or segment
	Creating a new product line
	Developing a new technology (or new type of system)

needs are satisfied by the project. For one group, a project may be a huge success, but for another, a total failure.

- **Success criteria must be prioritized.** Success criteria can be conflicting, which means there will often be trade-offs that must be agreed to by all parties before the project is started. In many projects there may be a large number of stakeholders, consequently there is a need to identify the stakeholders who are going to have the most influence in determining project success. Their criteria should have a higher priority and should be emphasized (Lipovertsky et al. 1997).
- **Success is affected by time.** Each success criterion has its own timescale for measurement. For example, time and budget aspects can be measured as soon as a project is completed, whereas product usefulness may only become clear after several years.
- **Success may be partial.** Project success may be partially achieved, or projects may be measured in varying degrees of success. The determination of project success can be ambiguous and it becomes extremely difficult to give an unequivocal verdict of success or failure when some criteria are successfully met, and others are not.

Common reasons for the failure of technology projects

Mobile working is a very new sub-discipline of Information Technology/Information Systems (IT/IS) enabled change so there is no specific research available. For this reason I am using general IT project-related literature in this chapter. IT has changed almost every aspect of our life, but there are strong indications to suggest that not all IT projects are successful. Doherty et al. (2000) argue that few information systems can be considered a success. The reason for claiming success, they argue, is largely based on erroneous methods of measuring success. These methods they say are usually focused on the extent to which a system meets the requirement specification agreed at the start of a project. The main measures of success are often negative in nature, namely the so-called correspondence failure whereby the system objectives are stated in advance, and failure is defined in terms of these objectives having been achieved or not achieved. Lyytinen and Hirschheim (1987) suggest the notion of expectation failure or the failure of the system to meet the expectations of stakeholders and propose four dimensions of failure (presented in Table 7.2).

Having mentioned the types of failure, it is also important to briefly cover some of the most common causes of the IS projects failure and most of these would also apply to mobile working projects. Different researchers and practitioners give different reasons for these failures and these opinions are summarized in Table 7.3.

In most instances, the systems development life cycle emerges, implicitly or explicitly, as an important control element, resulting in success measures adhering to the functional engineering model, taking a structured, problem-solving approach: human complexity in the system is viewed as something which can be analysed for which a requirement specification can be written. But many disagree with this view. Beath and Orlykowski (1994), for example, criticize the interaction between users and system professionals when systems are built, and argue that users' participation is seen as ideological rather than actual, with users often taken to be passive rather than active stakeholders in the process.

As discussed in the previous section, just like success, failure could also be a matter of perception if the success measures were not clearly spelt out right at the start of the project. Some of the common reasons for project failures are outlined below.

Organizational structure: Deficiencies in the apparent organizational structure such as a lack of a performance-measuring subsystem or a control/decision-making subsystem can cause major problems in project management (Fortune and White, 2006). There are many different types of organizational structures: bureaucratic, hierarchical and matrix methods are the most commonly cited. Jackson and Schuler (1995) suggest alternative views of organizations and look at four particular views: organizations as machines, organisms, cultures and coercive systems. A mechanistic view takes organizations as machines, within which rule-based systems can be used to control operations in a controlled manner. So if the inputs to the process are known, the outputs can be predicted with a fair degree of precision.

An organization as an organism is seen from a system's perspective. The organization is a collection of sub-systems organized to maintain a 'steady state' within their environment. Organizations as cultures see their functioning as a social structure. In this view, there are no fixed structures and the composition of people changes to reflect business objectives. Finally, organizations seen as coercive systems are viewed as functioning according to power structures, adding a unique element which is not present in the other three views. This view promotes the notion that organizations support the status quo or maintain existing power structures. Mobile working projects are often about re-organizing the business operations and re-structuring so this view of an organization is only useful in determining how to tackle the status quo.

There are some other ideas on organizational structures, such as Mintzberg (1998), which suggest that organizations are subject to seven forces; direction, proficiency, innovation, concentration, efficiency, co-operation and competition. Detailed discussion of these structures is outside the scope of this chapter and a flavour of thinking about organizational structures given here demonstrates both the complexity of the situation under which the mobile working projects have to be managed and the problems present in organizational structures, such as too many layers and extreme politics, which can have an influence on the project's success or failure.

Lack of clear purpose: Objectives were not clear at the beginning or became blurred in the passage of time. This can happen especially in large projects which are completed over a long period of time. Over a prolonged period organizational priorities can change or lack of clarity about long-term objectives may come about, leading to a push of the project in the wrong direction.

Setting unrealistic targets: This issue is one of the most common causes of a project failure. Project objectives should be: set with realistic estimates of time and resources available, specific and measurable descriptions of a specific performance objective, descriptive of the intended result in regard to "how much or what by when", jointly agreed and prioritized with consultation with stakeholders and set at the beginning of the project while being reviewed regularly to ensure they remain realistic and relevant.

Lack of communication: Communication is not clear between different stakeholders or groups of stakeholders. This is often the case in technology-related projects where managers do not understand the technology and technologists do not understand the business, resulting in misinterpretation of objectives/requirements.

Lack of proper planning: Without proper and detailed planning it is easy to underestimate the time or resources required to achieve desired objectives. Successful deployment of IT projects should be based within, and guided by, a realistic timeframe. Often the timescale for a project will be too short and as a result, projects overrun. This may come to be seen as a failure and in some cases may lead to abandonment (Procaccino, 2005).

Misunderstanding of the environment: Due consideration not given to the environment under which the project will be managed or the product will be used. This could lead to insufficient resources or efforts allocated to deal with the environmental factors. In the mobile working context, most output devices such as laptops

TABLE 7.2 Types of information systems failure (adapted from Lyytinen and Hirschheim, 1987)

Failure type	Explanation
Correspondence	The failure of the final 'system' to correspond with the requirements/objectives determined in advance
Process	Failure in the development process, usually in the form of a cost/time overrun or inability to complete the development
Interaction	Users fail to use the 'system' sufficiently or effectively, meaning it has failed
Expectation	Failure of the completed 'system' to meet the expectations of participants

TABLE 7.3 Some of the most common causes of the IS project failure (adopted from Avison and Torkzadeh, 2009)

Failure factors	Examples
Human Issues	Employee turnover – People leaving the project and it's often hard to find suitable replacements
	Conflicts – Between individual, teams, departments or outsourcing partners
	Motivation – Lack of motivation during development or at usage stage
Technical Issues	Hardware and software issues such as difficulties in integration, scalability or robustness
	Data integration issues due to format difference or transfer limitations as data suitable for mobile devices may be different from the data used in traditional PCs
Political Issues	Too much competition between different stakeholders to gain rewards
	Too much or too little control/authority
	Conflicts in terms of expected benefits/project objectives
Financial Issues	Errors in estimates
	Poor budget control
	Cost overruns
Lack of Leadership	Lack of vision and ability to inspire
	Poor people, technology or processes management

or tablets will be used outdoors where sunlight could make it difficult to see things on screens clearly. These environmental factors must be taken into account if project failure is to be prevented.

Poor requirement specifications: Vague specifications often affect project success. Mobile working projects are often complex, but initial specifications may sometimes be vague and unclear. This may result in a relative lack of progress in the deployment of the systems.

Imbalance of priorities: An imbalance between the resources applied to the basic transformation processes and those allocated to the related monitoring and control processes, leading to quality problems or cost increases or delays (Fortune and White 2006). In a mobile working project, too many resources may be allocated to the technologies (hardware and software) and too few to the organizational change which can result in project failures.

Scope creep: Clients sometimes have additional demands after a project contract is finalized or even when a project is close to completion which may be beyond the scope or resources allocated to the project. This, in many instances, can hamper project progress. When design changes cause plan and schedule changes, the problem is more complicated than merely modifying the design.

Lack of support from top management: Technology projects have high uncertainty in terms of time/cost and objectives attached to them (Avison and Torkzadeh, 2010). Therefore support from top management is essential to deal with problems resulting from uncertainty such as cost or time overruns.

Poor project control: In many cases, management wants to avoid change and hence faces paradoxical situations when change occurs. This may be counter-productive to project success. Changing requirements however should be managed by having flexibility built into the initial project plans and sufficient resources allocated.

Lack of good leadership: Projects go through many good and bad periods and require good leadership skills to keep all stakeholders motivated and plans on track. If a project is underestimated in terms of time, resources or level of organizational change, it usually falls under the responsibility of junior managers. The lack of a good leader with power to obtain necessary resources can easily cause projects to fail.

Poor testing: Tests, conducted during project planning, may be incomprehensive and incomplete. This is common with regard to planning project finances. Project managers are often satisfied if they have a fixed source of funds and may not want to explore other options. The problem occurs when committed sources of funds face challenges and fail to deliver according to their promises (Coley, 2006). Poor testing can also be a major problem in technological projects when a number of bugs are left in the systems and it fails to perform when exposed to the pressures of a real business environment. Software bugs are not the only problem requiring testing: scalability and adoptability of systems must also be thoroughly tested.

Lack of user participation: New technologies often face resistance from most user groups which includes employees as well as customers. Technical projects require all users of the system to be involved. Lack of user involvement and stakeholder participation may hamper the success. It is not an easy issue to deal with, especially when users are customers and both hierarchical structures and top-down management practices may often come in the way of desirable levels of user involvement.

Unsupportive organizational culture: A project can fail if the project team, the system it is developing or desired outcome do not fit well in their organization's culture. Organizational culture can be described as the collective will or consciousness of an organization, based on certain patterns of beliefs shared by all its members. Culture emerges from the social interaction of all organizational members.

When developing and implementing IS, culture needs to be understood so that an organization is in a better position to incorporate its IS strategies which are in line with the existing culture and any cultural change is seen to be in progress.

This essentially emergent view presented by Clarke (2007) sees culture as embedded in the symbols, myths, ideologies and rituals of the organization (Figure 7.4). Symbols are the shared codes of meaning within the organization, and may appear as language (particularly evident in information technology), corporate offices, company car schemes, logos or simply stories about the organization that are passed down over the years. Myths are evident in all organizations, commonly appearing as founder myths or creation myths. The ideology is an organization's system of knowledge or set of beliefs about the social world, key among which will be their ethical position. Too often, organizations are seen to have one ideology, whereas actually, all organizations have sets of consonant and conflicting ideologies. Rituals within organizations help to cement the underlying values. Most sales conventions have acceptable behaviours and dress codes which are not prescribed, but are known and followed: wear a suit and tie; clean your company car; support some speakers and not others, etc. To be successful at implementing a project with far reaching implications, the organization needs to determine what its 'culture' is, how it is changing and where the major influences are coming from.

Insufficient attention to change management: Managing change is difficult and complex. Change management is dominated by 'manipulative' assumptions, with cultural factors, through which an organization deals with the underlying beliefs. Early approaches to dealing with human issues, in which the views of participants were seen as barriers to be overcome, have partially given way to a cultural perspective through which change is perceived as a participative rather than a planned or structured process. There is a need to combine methods aimed at dealing with change from both planning (revolutionary or transformational) and incremental (evolutionary) perspectives. In particular, whilst evolutionary change is valuable in the short to medium term, revolutionary change may be necessary in the longer term and may be hampered by an evolutionary or incremental process.

Typical steps in an IS project

All technology projects will have unique features in terms of size, market environment, technological or organizational change needs. Having said that, they will also have a number of common aspects and the following is a guide to the typical phases such a mobile working project will go through.

Feasibility study: Top management is convinced that a new mobile working system will bring many benefits to the organization but is not clear about return on investment (ROI), suitability/ability of the organization to take such a giant step or availability of required resources, so they conduct a feasibility study to address these issues.

Decision to go ahead: This decision is often taken by the top management if the results of the feasibility study are convincing, followed up by initial top-level plans.

User requirements definition: Conducting surveys and interviews with users which will be used to determine project requirements.

Risk analysis: The risk analysis will be carried out in collaboration with all involved departments. It will produce a risk management plan which will be used to manage risks of mobile working implementation.

Project planning: Detailed project plans are created for the development of systems, testing, deployment and handover. Dealing with organizational change management issues will also be planned at this stage.

Pilot project: Pilot systems to be developed and evaluated to refine project plans and systems requirements.

System development: The relevant systems will be developed in house or by the outsourcing vendor under the guidance of an organization. The organization and the outsourcing vendor often conduct the acceptance/functionality testing jointly.

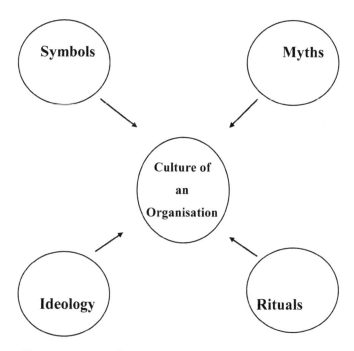

FIGURE 7.4 The components of organisational culture
(adapted from Clarke, 2007)

Training: Training in the use of new technologies as well as operations will be managed by all parties involved. The training will be conducted in parallel to most phases of the project but are to be completed before services go live.

Evaluating: Regular evaluations are required especially at the beginning of the services going live to address any problems, to assess benefits and to learn from the experience so that the next iteration brings better results.

Project management methodologies/tools

A typical project will involve hundreds of activities which would roughly fall into the following categories.

- Cost estimating and preparing budgets.
- Planning for effective communication and deciding on which communication tools will be used. Some project management tools such as PRINCE2 offer group working facilities to enable effective team working.
- Setting goals for individuals and project teams.
- Implementing change and process improvement.
- Quality assurance and controls.
- Risk assessment and management.

- Scheduling and time management, etc.

Without a proper project methodology, different stakeholders such as top management, project managers, users and workers, etc., will have different ideas about how things should be organized and when the different parts of the project will be completed. All stakeholders need to know how much responsibility, authority and accountability they have, and due to the complexity involved in mobile working projects, there will often be confusion surrounding these issues. The project management methodologies help plan and keep track of the above mentioned activities. A good project management method can guide the project through a controlled, well-managed, visible set of activities to achieve the desired results. There are many project management methodologies/tools but the most commonly used include PRINCE2 and Microsoft Project.

PRINCE2

PRINCE2, or **PR**ojects **IN** **C**ontrolled **E**nvironments, is a comprehensive methodology for project management. It was developed and owned by the Office of Government and Commerce (OGC) in the UK. PRINCE2 has a dedicated accreditation body (APM Group Ltd) with over 15 accelerated consulting organizations.

PRINCE2 describes eight components which need to be present for a successful project (Murray, 2008):

- **Business case:** The business reasons/objectives for the project.
- **Organization:** Helping in planning the roles and responsibilities of the stakeholders.
- **Plans:** Defining the project's products, how the work should be carried out, when and by whom.
- **Controls:** How the project managers exercise control.
- **Management of risk:** Identification and management of risk.
- **Quality in a project environment:** Management of quality issues and procedures.
- **Configuration management:** How the project's products are developed and configured.
- **Change control:** How to manage changes to specification or scope of the project/product.

PRINCE2 can provide projects with:

- A controlled and organized start, middle and end.
- Regular reviews of progress against the plan and against the business objectives.
- Flexible decision points.
- Automatic management control of any deviations from the plan.
- The involvement of management and stakeholders at the right time during the project

- Good communication channels between the project management team and the rest of the organization.
- Agreement on the required quality at the outset and continuous monitoring against those requirements.

PRINCE2 is a process-driven methodology rather than a rigidly staged one, so it offers the systematic flexibility required for mobile working projects. PRINCE2 contains a complete set of concepts and project management processes that are necessary for a properly run and managed project. However, the way in which PRINCE2 is applied to each project will vary considerably and tailoring the method to suit the circumstances of a particular project is critical to its successful use.

Microsoft Project

This is another common project management methodology as well as a software tool. It is a useful and popular project management tool used for business project planning, scheduling tasks, managing resources, monitoring costs and generating reports. Its main features include:

- help in defining the content and the building of the project plan;
- a calendar to reflect the work schedule;
- aiding allocation of tasks;
- added sub-tasks, linked related tasks and set task dependencies;
- milestones to identify significant events;
- information lag and lead times and constraining dates;
- a resource list and created resource calendars for the resources;
- a critical path to reflect the core project processes;
- comprehensive reporting tools to keep track of the progress.

The latest version of MS Project called MS Project Professional 2010 (see Microsoft. com) is easy to use and very comprehensive in terms of its coverage of different aspects of project management. The user interface is similar to the widely used MS Office Suite and every day project management tasks such as resources control and communication between different stakeholders are fairly easy to undertake.

There are other tools to complement these methodologies and details of such tools can be obtained from www.pmi.org or other related websites. In addition to these tools/methods, we also recommend a system 'approach to project management' see Clarke (2007) for an example of its implementation, which can be used in conjunction with the above described tools/techniques.

A Systems approach to project management

It has been argued earlier that mobile working is a complex domain and the management of systems might be seen as attempts to control variety and complexity through a reductionist approach. Reductionism seeks to understand systems in terms of their constituent parts, assuming that these parts operate independently. This approach, which sees organizations as rigid structures with departments working in an isolated manner, is not suitable for large organizations with their mix of professionals working towards common objectives but often within fairly loose forms of organization. This approach is especially undesirable in a mobile working environment where systems and organizational integration is vital for success. Here, a more holistic and systemic approach might be seen as more likely to be successful and such an approach is fundamental in systems approaches to project management.

The central idea behind system thinking is that organizations are constituted of sub-systems or elements that are in interrelationships with one another and which exist within a boundary. What is important is not the elements per se, but the interrelationships between them, because it is the nature of the interrelationships that gives character to the system. Inputs to the system are transformed within it and go out as output, which in turn informs further input with feedback (Figure 7.5).

Organizations constantly interact with their environment and modern modes of working mean that often, members of organizations work as temporary networks, multi-disciplinary and virtual teams and sometimes even as temporary organizations in themselves for the achievement of particular business objectives.

The environment outside the system is regularly a challenge to be addressed by the variety within it. The discipline of cybernetics (Ashby, 1956) has forwarded the idea that variety can only be addressed with variety. Organizations normally create departments to deal with specific business aspects like sales, personnel, marketing, procurement, finance and so on. The danger is that these departments can become closed systems operating in isolation, not interacting with one another. As a result of this, more often than not, short-term project goals are maximized at the cost of long-term interests of an organization. In effective organizations, people have to work across departments in a systemic way so that planning is done with a holistic perspective of where the organization currently is and what it wants to achieve. In the project management field, this process is sometimes called programme management. For instance, Xerox, the first company in the US to win back market share from the Japanese in the 1980s (Guns, 1996), adopted a new strategy to fight Japanese competition. The then CEO of Xerox, Allaire, split the company into eight divisions, each focusing on a particular product or a product group (Guns, 1996). This was probably an attempt to overcome departmental barriers and provide a product-specific platform, bringing together members of different departments to share diverse knowledge and work together for a specific product or common organizational objectives.

Systems thinking promotes the understanding that departments may contain boundaries, but not barriers. Whereas boundaries allow the permeation of ideas and opinion and facilitate team working, barriers do not. Hence, while boundaries can be facilitative, barriers are prohibitive. Perception plays a crucial role here as it basically depends upon the observer who perceives what causes the system to work together. Therefore, the systems thinker is continually negotiating and re-negotiating through boundary critique: a process where organizational knowledge as well as its environment may be continuously synthesized.

Systems thinking can provide significant philosophical and practical underpinnings for technological projects. IS needs to be perceived as a network of activities, rather than as stand-alone technological projects managed by the IT department. For effective planning and deployment of systems, people should work across departments forming networks, the members of which can then be aided in thinking more systemically about the organization as a whole, instead of perceiving their own responsibilities in an isolated manner. Non-systemic ways of working within an organization, defined by departmental and other barriers, could result in failure of the whole project. This is particularly true of mobile working projects where businesses almost always have to be re-structured and operations change considerably.

Managing project risks

There are a large number of risks associated with mobile working projects. Risks need to be identified at the planning stage and a risk log should be created as early in the planning stage as possible. A risk log is created at the beginning of the project along with a project brief. Each risk identified should have its own number, the type of risk and a summary of its status and analysis. There should be an owner, amongst senior staff, for every risk.

The risk log is used to identify all risks, their likelihood, consequences and result/impact on the project. At the beginning of the project, the risk log, along with all information from the project brief and approach are used to determine the justifications of the project. These are revised at every stage to determine: new risks, if we should continue and if the risks climbing, and finally, assess at the end of the project, any remaining risks to the operational system.

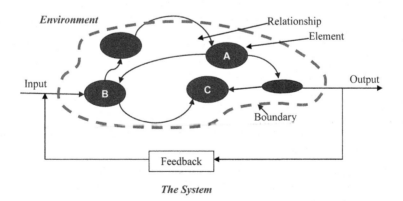

FIGURE 7.5 The systems perspective
(adapted from Flood and Jackson, 1991)

The risk analysis stage should be broken into five types: **prevention** (i.e. don't do it), reduction (what can be done to reduce it, at what cost?), **transference** (can someone else do it better?), **contingency** (what do we need, should this happen?) and **acceptance** (can we live with it or may it be unlikely to happen or too expensive).

Risk Management includes planning for the risk (identify countermeasures), identifying any resources needed to counter the risk, monitoring the risk for early warnings and assessing it for any impact of changes, etc. All risks should be controlled to make the plan happen.

Managing human issues

A mobile working project will have significant economic, organizational and social impacts on the organization. Therefore, well-defined goals combined with a communication strategy will reduce any resentment amongst the organizations's staff. Such resentment may create a negative atmosphere that will have considerable consequences on the progress of the project.

In multinational companies, cultural differences often exacerbate communication problems. For example, a text message from someone where communication tends to be more direct might seem rude to someone from a different background. Misalignment of expectations can be the source of major problems in large-scale projects. To avoid such mishaps, we suggest ongoing communication to manage each other's expectations. Communication can build trust and this greater trust can often lead to an improvement on formal and informal communication levels. Hence, meaningful communication is a necessary antecedent of trust. There are two types of communication: formal and informal. Formal communication is often about hard data such as legal, technical or commercial data. Informal communication is more personal and requires a greater degree of trust and understanding between different stakeholders in a project.

Mobile working projects often result in a significant impact on the organization and require people throughout the organization to learn new behaviours and skills. Negative effects of change are inevitable when people are forced to adjust to fast-paced change. Organizations need to proactively recognize the effects of change and develop skills among staff to enable the change. Without this proactive approach, the risk of resistance to change increases significantly and reduces the chances of achieving expected benefits. The topic of change management is discussed in the next chapter in greater detail.

Chapter summary

It is becoming increasingly common to manage the organization and in particular, strategic change, through projects or project portfolios, called programme management. Mobile working is often considered a major change and requires careful management of its projects.

A very high number of technological projects fail because of poor project management. To gain competitive advantage and create value through adoption of change management strategies, companies can implement business processes that allow efficient and effective enterprise project management.

It is important to understand that success in projects is largely a subjective concept. Any success evaluation should take into account both the hard (tangible and measurable) and soft (subjective and difficult to quantify) dimensions of success. Success is perceived differently by different stakeholders and success criteria must be prioritized to address any possible conflicts. Success is also affected by time, with some measures being short-term and others long-term. Success may be partial, as some criteria may be successfully met whilst others may not.

Project managers must agree the criteria with the stakeholders as early as possible and apply appropriate factors to deliver agreed dimensions of success. The rate of success may also be improved if all parties involved keep expectations at a realistic level and place importance on a quality product and organizational congruency. Focused use of configuration management, change control processes and quality review processes with user involvement throughout should ensure that all acceptance criteria are achieved and measured.

To be successful, any complex project needs to work across departments at both the planning and operational levels. The mobile working project needs to address long-term organizational benefit and sustainability as well as short-term gains. There is a difference between seeing the separation of departments as barriers to interaction and seeing them as boundaries to be permeated. Staff from different departments need to be brought together with the view of working towards common objectives. Stakeholders' participation in decision making from the earliest stages of a project is needed to ensure that there is a common will to collaborate rather than resistance to open up.

8

CHANGE MANAGEMENT

Case study: LondonWaste

This case study was prepared by the author to facilitate class discussion rather than illustrate effective or ineffective management practices. Only publicly available material has been used to write this case and it does not reflect any opinions of employees or management at this organization.

LondonWaste (LWL) is a public private partnership. The company is half owned by the North London Waste Authority (NLWA) which is a consortium of seven North London boroughs. The other 50 per cent shareholder is the waste management company, SITA UK. At present, the company provides waste disposal services for the NLWA, covering the boroughs of Barnet, Camden, Enfield, Islington, Hackney, Haringey and Waltham Forest. They also handle commercial, confidential, green and clinical waste for a range of customers including businesses, hospitals and non-profit organizations. Since its formation in 1994, LondonWaste has developed into one of the Capital's largest waste management companies, handling over 1 million tonnes of waste a year. It offers a broad range of services to clients including recycling, waste treatment and disposal (Source: *Computer Weekly*, 6 June 2005).

LondonWaste's senior management and sales staff spend prolonged periods of time away from the office. In particular, some of its managers spend longer periods of time than deemed normal on the road, travelling to meet with customers that are based further afield. LondonWaste approached a vendor and asked for a mobile data solution that would enable these executives to remain in touch with the office while on the move. The decision was taken for London-Waste's executives to be equipped with handsets and a mobile email solution.

A key concern for LondonWaste was to reduce the cost of fines levied on the company when its vehicles used routes that were not allocated to the company for waste collection. LondonWaste implemented a mobile data solution which was available to make its fleet management system more efficient. The solution was installed in-vehicle to enable LondonWaste to track 32 of its waste collection vehicles, enabling it to record whether its fleet stay on the appropriate allocated routes.

Benefits of mobile working include:

- Executives have noticed immediate productivity benefits in being able to access and respond to emails in real-time and on the move.
- It has enabled LondonWaste to manage and control costs incurred by its waste collection fleet.
- LondonWaste has received positive commendations from its senior executives and mobile staff in providing services that have made their business lives more manageable and effective.

In terms of timescales, LondonWaste first started implementing the mobile email solution in September 2003 and the system was securely set up and running by December in the same year.

Introduction

Building on the organization issues discussed in Chapter six, this chapter discusses the key issues in change management, and common approaches/methods to managing technology-related organizational change will be outlined. The question of how these approaches can be specifically used in mobile working projects will also be discussed.

Change management is a well-developed concept in literature and a number of methods exist for managing technology-related changes. The most common themes include:

- Create a vision to inspire people.
- Create a plan to manage change.
- Communicate exact changes to affected parties.
- Motivate and empower stakeholders using training as well as incentives to embrace change.
- Cement the change in the organization's culture gradually.

The management of social issues must be taken seriously as the mismanagement of these issues is often cited as a key reason for the failure of these projects.

Change management issues

One of the main problems established organizations encounter when considering mobile working adoption is managing organizational change in a way that people feel part of the change and help deliver business objectives. Achieving this, however, is not very easy and there are number of problematic issues which are discussed in this section.

Technology adoption is usually slow if too much attention is paid to technical aspects rather than business processes and social issues. Some companies sell their mobile working projects as 'pilot' or 'learning' vehicles and leave its development to the IT department. Many senior executives also equate 'going mobile' with a specific technology in mind rather than using suitable technologies to implement their organization's strategic objectives. Going mobile is about serving customers better, creating innovative products/services, leveraging organizational talent, achieving significant improvements in productivity and increasing revenues. The high start-up cost of mobile working also causes some organizations to delay its implementation. Lack of a well-defined strategy that is aligned with general business strategy is also one of the most common problems. To minimize the effects of these issues a mobile working initiative, just like any other business project, should be undertaken within a strategic framework.

Change management projects have very poor success rates. Organizational change is a dynamic process encompassing different but interrelated forms of diversity. This diversity might be related to several dimensions such as organizational structure and culture or the interactions between different dimensions of an organization. Causes of failures can often be found in inefficient interactions of: technical and human activities, the organization with its environment or unsuitable organizational design and management style. Lack of systematic change management methodologies or problems in their implementation is another commonly cited problem. Most of the change management methodologies focus on four common dimensions of an organization (process, design, culture and politics).

Process change may involve changing service development process (from market research to actual roll out) cash flow (from investments to profits), human resource input and information flow. Structural change involves changes to organizational functions, the organization of their counterparts, co-ordination and control, for example, changes in horizontal and vertical structures; in the decision systems or policy and resource allocation mechanisms; and in the processes used for recruitment, appraisal, compensation and career development. Culture encompasses such issues as values, beliefs and human behaviour in terms of mutual relationships and social norms. Politics may involve the power of change makers or those who resist it, or it may address the question of which stakeholders will be affected and why, etc.

The above categorization is useful in the understanding of diversity in organizational change as well as interaction between these dimensions. The four types of organizational change are interconnected through a dynamic process, so a change in any one dimension will result in changes in others. Therefore an initiative to carry out changes to one or two areas in isolation is likely to fail.

Cao and Cao (1999) suggested a generic critical model with four interrelated types of organizational change:

- Process change—change in flows and controls over flows. Typical approaches may include Total Quality Management (TQM) and Business Process Reengineering

(BPR). BPR is more relevant to mobile working as business processes often need re-engineering if they are to be delivered in a mobile mode. TQM can also be used to design and assess services effectiveness.

- Structural change—change in functions, their organization, co-ordination and control. Typical approaches include contingency theory, transaction cost economics and the configuration approach. These are reported in literature to improve the efficiency and effectiveness of the more tangible sides of an organization, but are impoverished in dealing with human centred issues (Cao and Frank, 2001).
- Cultural change—change in values, beliefs and human behaviour in terms of relationship to social rules and practices. Two of the main cultural approaches are unitary culture (Kotter, 1996) and cultural diversity management (Cox and Blake, 1991). These approaches force attention to the human side of organizations.
- Political change—change in power distribution and the way organizational issues are influenced. These can be associated with the political models of organization, developed by Pugh (1978), Mintzberg (1998), Morgan (1997), Pfeffer (1992, 1994), and Pettigrew (1985). In these models, the focus is on power, domination, political bargaining and the negotiation processes.

A holistic view of the four types of organizational change is based on this classification.

The four-dimensional view of organizational change implies that managing organizational change needs diversity in approaches. Each of the four types of organizational change are the sources of a particular type of problem so it needs four categories of change management approaches to deal with different types of organizational change. These approaches might be needed to work simultaneously or at different stages of the overall change process in a mobile working project.

Each part of the change management approach is primarily focused on a specific type of organizational change. Therefore, these approaches lack the power to deal with situations where more than one type of organizational change is required. Since different types of organizational change are interrelated, they need to be managed together through a holistic approach. This requires that multiple methods and/or methodologies are applied to a single change context. Whichever change approach or approaches are being followed, there is the need to critically evaluate whether the change is being implemented effectively. Systems thinking, which is covered in other chapters of this book in greater details, therefore, has a clear relevance to holistic change management. It better enables a holistic approach to organizational problem contexts which it sees as interdependent sub systems within the larger organizational system.

One such holistic approach (See Table 8.1) called Management of Change (MOC) is suggested by Cao and Cao (1999) which relates the four types of organizational change to the three different systemic approaches: Hard Systems Thinking (HST), Soft Systems Thinking (SST) and Critical Systems Thinking (CST). The objective is to help practitioners in analysing and addressing diversity in organizational change both systemically and critically. The key idea of the MOC framework is to help manage the diversity and interactions in organizational change and the change

TABLE 8.1 Systematic framework for the management of change (adapted from Cao et al. 1999)

	Hard systems thinking	Soft systems thinking	Critical systems thinking
Process	Efficient process design and change	Interpreting the ideas, beliefs and values underpinning the process design and change	Challenging the ideas, beliefs and values underpinning the process to achieve better balance
Structural	Efficient design of vertical and horizontal structure, decision systems and human resources system	Interpreting the ideas, beliefs and values underpinning the structure design and change	Challenging the ideas, beliefs and values underpinning the design of organisations to develop efficient structures
Cultural	Strong culture development	Encouraging diverse ideas, values and beliefs	Challenging dominant ideas, values and beliefs to reveal who is disadvantaged
Political	Conflicts of different values and interests are minimised by legally accepted power	Conflicts of different values and interests are balanced through various sources of power	Revealing coercive influences and effects, improving the positions of the disadvantaged

management methods. The framework is explicitly based on CST and is intended to help through a critical process, determining the organizational change context, scope, participative issues and the use of multiple methods to facilitate and inform decision-making related to change management.

The power of this approach lies in its ability to relate different change management methods to each other through a systemic framework. The framework represents something deeper than just the use of different methods to address (say) a mixed process/cultural context: it actually enables the managers applying it to see a single context differently. For example, if a change management problem is process specific, HST can provide general principles for the effective and efficient design of organizational processes, focusing most likely on approaches such as BPR and TQM. But what if there are different views about implementing this change process? In this case, SST can be utilised to help gain a better understanding of these views. Additionally, if there are disagreements where one view is dominating over others, CST may help reveal who will benefit from or be disadvantaged by the implementation of change (Cao and Cao, 1999).

Similarly with structural change, there is rarely a consensus on the design of vertical and horizontal organizational structures, decision systems and human resource systems, and SST can be used to help understand the values and beliefs underlying the change decisions, whilst CST can help uncover political issues of power and conflict.

Cultural change is particularly complex when implementing mobile working, as in the absence of a physical proximity, mobile employees tend to become disengaged from the organizational culture. Whilst HST might be useful in helping develop a unitary or strong organizational culture, such approaches must be used with care. It is all too easy to *assume* a consensus where in truth there is strict control over the expression of views. SST is more likely to be of value in a receptive environment for diverse ideas, values and beliefs, and thereby helping develop an ideas-rich organization. Where disagreements are found, with one view dominating, CST might at least help to understand, and at best, neutralize the dominant culture so that a diverse range of ideas also get attention.

This framework can be applied in practice to help develop a holistic view of the change context. What types of organizational changes are needed? What are the possible interactions between them? Is it possible that the one organizational change may result in other types of changes? This type of questioning aims to help develop a better understanding of the change situation.

The availability of too much information or advice can also be problem as stated here:

> Managers end up immersing themselves in an alphabet soup of initiatives. They lose focus and become obsessed by all the advice available in print and on-line about why organizations should change, what they should try to achieve and how they should do it. This proliferation of recommendations often leads to a confused approach and mixed results when change is attempted.
>
> *(Beer and Nohria, 2000)*

To manage these issues, a detailed change management strategy and plan is often required to facilitate the adoption process. This plan is likely to include detailed evaluation of which part of the organization and which employees are likely to be affected. A great deal of care will be needed in actual execution of change to minimize physical and emotional disruptions caused by the implementation of mobile working.

Old organizational structures are often a barrier to implementing the changes required for a dynamic service delivery channel, such as mobile working. To create a smooth and efficient experience for customers, business processes often need to be re-engineered and the number of management hierarchies reduced to speed up decision making. Changing an organization from a bureaucratic organization to an agile/responsive one opens up a number of risks; ones which should be managed with careful change management.

A key strategy for the success of mobile working is to promote innovation in organizations. There are many ways in which innovation can be promoted in an organization including: creating room for experiments, tolerance to the failure of good ideas, implementing a reward system to encourage individuals as well as teams to innovate. Some concepts such as 'absorptive capacity' and 'complexity studies' see knowledge as the key enabler in organizational innovation. Absorptive capacity is about measuring an organization's ability to value, assimilate and apply new knowledge. Measuring is done at multiple levels (individual, group, firm and national level) (Zahra and George, 2002). 'Complexity studies' are derived from general systems theory and regard innovation as the continuity and transformation of patterns of interaction, understood as complex responses of humans relating to one another in local situations (Fonseca, 2001). These frameworks help organizations to understand the usefulness of information, assimilate it through systematic interactions and apply it to achieve success at innovation through technology.

There are also many barriers to innovation, including: short-term results-oriented culture, resistance to change and low acceptance rates of new ideas. In a mobile working environment, the speed of new innovations may overwhelm many employees and proper change management strategies become more important here compared to conventional situations.

Effects of these barriers can be minimized by promotion of an innovation culture in organizations.

Trust

Traditionally, trust in new systems generally meant a secure system, but according to Chankar *et al.* (2002), perceptions of trust have steadily evolved from being a construct involving security and privacy issues on the Internet (which is often used as communication platform for mobile workers), to a multi-dimensional, complex construct that includes reliability and credibility, emotional comfort and quality for multiple stake-holders such as employees, suppliers, distributors and regulators, in addition to customers.

The issue of trust building can be addressed in a number of ways. To start with a professional technical advisor in a dedicated call centre can do a lot to inspire confidence. When a stakeholder knows that somebody will be there to speak to if anything goes wrong in the mobile environment, he/she will have confidence in doing their job. Other factors, such as keeping system performance promises, providing comprehensive training and giving employees time to adjust to new work practices, always helps. Employees need assurances that their liability in the event of things going wrong will be limited, especially during the early days. In addition, organizations need to take active steps to further promote trust in mobile working. These steps may include:

- Being pro-active in combating corporate crimes and cooperating with other organizations and other regulatory/professional bodies to detect and prevent crimes.
- Taking proper care in protecting consumers' data and taking particular care in using it or keeping it on mobile devices.
- Providing appropriate guarantees against consumer losses in the event of a breach.

Ethical issues

Consideration of the ethics of mobile working have mainly focused on areas relating to the use/abuse of information held in mobile devices. In this context, the main issues may include security/privacy of information about individuals, accuracy of information, ownership of information and intellectual property, accessibility of information held and which uses of this information are ethically acceptable.

One of the main benefits of mobile working is that organizations can improve service and potentially generate more profits for shareholders and increase job security for employees. On the other hand, job losses are one of the methods for cutting costs and this has numerous negative implications for different stakeholders. The displacement of job opportunities away from a fixed work place into field-based mobile roles is a common feature of mobile working practice. This can cause considerable distress to some employees. How organizations deal with this issue often raises ethical issues which may be mitigated by a careful and considerate approach to change management.

Mobile working often causes loss of personal relationships between an organization and employees, dehumanizing the business process. An employee's relationship with an organization may have developed over years of loyal work. Reducing this to just mobile interaction and computer-generated responses and numbers/models would often result in a loss of the development of individual relationships, human touch and the use of intuition. Such aspects may be viewed as necessary to the new electronic economy, but human networks are just as important in terms of business practice as the efficiencies associated with mobile working.

Chapter summary

This chapter covered change-management-related factors associated with mobile working. Mobile working projects often cause revolutionary changes in organizational operations which cause considerable disruptions to employees' working patterns, mutual relationships and their relationship with both management and the organization as a whole.

Some of the problematic issues in managing change when implementing mobile working include:

- a lack of proper integration of operations resulting in overlaps and frustrations in employees;
- a culture of achieving only short-term targets which often means ignoring social issues associated with the change;
- a lack of understanding and knowledge, within the organization about mobile working;
- difficulties in the personalization of work;
- a lack of understanding that the mobile working initiative is a business critical area and not just a technical issue.

Existing organizational structure and unwillingness to change amongst employees is also often seen as one of the biggest hurdles in the implementation of mobile working and this book recommends a carefully planned and implemented change management strategy to manage this.

These concerns are generic and reasonably well known. It is important that institutions embarking on mobile working are fully aware of them, so that strategies can be developed to minimise their adverse effects. Additionally, each institution has its own set of organizational barriers that it needs to deal with.

9

SUMMARY, CONCLUSIONS AND RECOMMENDATIONS

Summary

This book set out to present various aspects of mobile working. At the beginning, review objectives were stated along with the definition of key terms. The second chapter described some of the main mobile devices such as 3G phones, PDAs and Bluetooth as well as technologies such as WiFi along with connectivity and access issues. The third chapter dealt with 'what is mobile working' and types of mobile workers such as blue collar workers and white collar workers. It also covered some of the major benefits of mobile working, for instance: flexibility, productivity, cost savings and drawbacks such as social problems and technology limitations. Chapter four illustrated some real world cases of mobile working implementations. Chapter five was a discussion of the key issues related to mobile working, for example, organizational issues, social issues, technology limitations, technology acceptance and cost benefit, etc.

Issues of how mobile working projects should be managed were also addressed along with the most common methods which could be used. Structured methodologies such as PRINCE2 and Microsoft Project were briefly summarized as they provide structure to managing the implementation of mobile working.

Mobile working implementations cause dramatic changes in business operations and as a result, the way in which employees work and interact with an organization changes too. Therefore, change must be managed by using well established change management methodologies with considerable resources and organizational energy allocated to managing social issues.

Conclusions

The above chapters show many gaps in mobile working practice. Below is a brief overview of lessons learnt from the mobile working projects so far:

- **Business problems that mobile working will address?** At present it seems that advances in mobile technologies are making existing mobile work forces such as utility, sales and transport workers more efficient and productive, but there is little knowledge about the other traditionally non-mobile areas of businesses. Mobile working models are likely to have significant impacts on most business problems especially from operations management and some of the issues covered in this book are relevant to all businesses.
- **Business opportunities that mobile working could create?** Many organizations have begun to think about the business opportunities created by mobile working. New and innovative models are being tried and tested. A key lesson so far is that although mobile working can provide solutions to many efficiency-related problems, it is by no means a solution to every problem, and businesses must think hard about their core competencies and capabilities before embarking on mobile working.
- **Potential risks:** There are many risks associated with the implementation of mobile working. Security threats and costs outstripping benefits are two commonly cited risks, whereas limitations in mobile technologies and users' resistance to accept new technology and working practices stand out as the most visible barriers to mobile working growth.
- **Potential advantages:** There are many advantages such as performance enhancement and higher productivity in mobile working, but most of these gains have been made by workforces who are already mobile such as sales or repair engineers. Benefits to the traditionally non-mobile work settings are still mixed and unclear.
- **What types of changes are likely to be needed?** Early indications are that organizations will need to change their business processes, ways in which information is provided and accessed, working practices, work relationships, working styles and most importantly, changes in roles, responsibilities and management structures. In practice, it often means a revolutionary change and thus, should be treated accordingly.
- **Skills and competences are needed to become an effective mobile worker:** This question has two dimensions, competencies at individual level and competencies at organizational level. Both dimensions are important and organizations must evaluate themselves and their employees to determine whether they have enough competencies to undergo such a big change.
- **Productivity gains from mobile working:** While many organizations experience considerable productivity gains, this mainly applies to workforces who are already mobile which have greatly benefited from the advances in mobile technologies. Productivity gains or even savings from implementing mobile working are still a matter of hot debate.
- **Management changes required for effective mobile working:** Again, workforces who are already mobile have gained considerable benefits while only making small changes in management. In contrast, early signs are that significant changes in management practices may be required to be effective at mobilizing

non-mobile workers. This means that management structures have to be re-engineered to fully benefit from mobile working.

Recommendations

Set goals for mobile working

Many organizations have started mobile working without having a clear goal in mind. To succeed, this must be addressed. For example, if one wants to improve customer service, reduce costs or improve efficiency, specific and measurable objectives for what one wants to achieve, such as improved productivity or increased sales, must be well thought-out. To get mobile technology right, it is important to start with a business aim rather than a technical solution. Therefore, the first step in any mobile project should be to ask what one wants to achieve, for instance: more contact with customers? Faster logistics? Better customer service? Once one has a business goal in mind, they should think about how mobile working could help to achieve this goal.

Address Social Issues

The workers that use mobile computing are a heterogeneous group. Those workers that are employed in a variable work context are even more diversified, considering that their work context changes often—many times within one workday. Their needs are also variable. It is important to understand and consider their work context, human characteristics and technical options available when designing mobile computing resources. Additionally, it is important to move beyond traditional modes of computing and discover alternative methods that could be developed to fulfil these needs. Most businesses keep the office space and maintain teams working in one location as much as possible, while allowing those workers who know and see each other regularly to take advantage of mobile working. Successful mobile working requires employees to feel that they are in control over their work schedule. However, this needs a new style of management and developing this is not always easy.

Mobile workers feel isolated at times and companies need to take a proactive approach to making sure the workers feel involved. There is a likelihood of losing context this way and losing body language, especially when one relies on email too much. People also tend to believe their colleagues don't trust them working mobile, when actually, many are overcompensating at home (McCue, 2005).

Evaluate options

Think about the way people in an organization work. Establish each of the potential mobile working employees and their communication needs. The following questions are examples of what should also be considered: is a business or staff artificially constrained by location or work space? Would staff welcome the opportunities of more flexible working? If a company has mobile staff or sales people, compare the new generation of mobile phones with PDAs and laptops: do they need to have a full PC or is receiving email enough?

Plan the rollout phase

Run a pilot test to see if a business benefits from the technology before investing heavily in any one technology. Look at training implications, such as what the cost will be and which staff will require training, and allow time for them to adjust to the new system. Also, will one have the technical expertise to install the technology oneself? And what about potential problems and ongoing maintenance? These are all question that need to be considered.

Monitor progress constantly

Organizations should regularly monitor and review the impact of mobile working on their business. They should get feedback from staff and suppliers on the changes to establish how to improve things further. As new technology is the key to mobile working, IT directors should work with human resources and business managers to understand the working culture and training issues that might impact on the use of technology Silicon (2005). The mobile computing architecture chosen should also compliment the work scenario and be understood by management so that it can be fully exploited to deliver desired business benefits.

APPENDIX

Glossary of terms used

Debit card   A debit card allows the account holders to access their funds in a current/ check account electronically. Debit cards may be used to obtain cash from automated teller machines or purchase goods or services using point-of-sale systems. The use of a debit card often involves immediate debiting and crediting of consumers' accounts.

Digital certificate The electronic equivalent of an ID card that authenticates the source of a digital signature.

Digital signatures A security option that uses two keys, one public and one private, which are used to encrypt messages before transmission and to decrypt them on receipt.

E-commerce   Conducting business using Internet.

Encryption   A data security technique used to protect information from unauthorized inspection or alteration. Information is encoded so that it appears as a meaningless string of letters and symbols during delivery or transmission. Upon receipt, the information is decoded using an encryption key.

Extended enterprise Information access to a wider, more dispersed group of workers.

HTML   Abbreviation for "Hypertext Markup Language." A set of codes that can be inserted into text files to indicate special typefaces, inserted images, and links to other hypertext documents.

Hyperlink   An item on a webpage that, when selected, transfers the user directly to another location in a hypertext document or to another webpage, perhaps on a different machine. Also simply called a "link".

Information management Describes the measures required for the effective collection, storage, access, use and disposal of information to support agency business processes. The core of these measures is the management of the definition, ownership, sensitivity, quality and accessibility of information. These measures are addressed at appropriate stages in the strategic planning lifecycle and applied at appropriate stages in the operational lifecycle of the information itself.

Information Systems (IS)	Organized collections of hardware, software, supplies, policies, procedures and people, which store, process and provide *access* to information.
Internet	A cooperative message-forwarding system linking computer networks all over the world.
Legacy systems	A term commonly used to refer to existing computers systems and applications with which new systems or applications must exchange information.
Mobile functionality	Ability to input data and get output in real time anytime, at desired locations.
Mobile working	It is different from simply remote working or home working. For the purpose of our research, mobile working means 'enabling workers to work away from home or the office by providing them with suitable mobile input/output devices'.
Mobile technology	Computing or connectivity devices, which can be carried easily from location to location.
MS Project	A project management methodology and a software tool to help manage the project.
Outsourcing	The practice of contracting with another entity to perform services that might otherwise be conducted in-house.
PRINCE2	A well-established project management methodology
Project	A task with specific objectives and pre-fixed timeline and resources
Programme Management	PRINCE2, or **PR**ojects **IN** **C**ontrolled **E**nvironments, is a comprehensive methodology for project management.
Website	The service of providing ongoing support and monitoring of an Internet-addressable computer that stores web pages and processes transactions initiated over the Internet.

REFERENCES

Abowd, G.D. (2002) The human experience. *Pervasive Computing,* 11, 48–57.

Agarwal, A., and Shankar, R. (2002) Analyzing alternatives for improvement in supply chain performance. *Work Study,* 51(1), 32–37.

Allan, L.S. and Andre, P.C. (2006) *Use of Mobile Technology and Intelligent Interfaces to Assist Contact Centres and Field Technicians.* http://www.nmmu.ac.za/documents/coe/ALeeson.pdf. Accessed: 3 January 2012.

Amato-McCoy, D.M. (2006) Planning for continuity. *Bank Systems & Technology.* February 27.

Antony, A. 2004, "A different mindset", *Personnel Today,* p. 29.

Armstrong, B. *et al.* (2010) Brain tumour risk in relation to mobile telephone use: results of the INTERPHONE international case-control study. *International Journal of Epidemiology,* 39(3): 675–694.

Ashby, W.R. (1956) *Introduction to Cybernetics.* London: Methuen. Available online at http://pespmc1.vub.ac.be/books/IntroCyb.pdf.

AT&T. (2011) *AT&T Security Consulting – Mobility Security Risk Assessment Services.* Available online at http://www.corp.att.com/consulting/docs/PB-cons_22609_V01_05–04-11.pdf. Accessed: 15 January 2012.

——(2011) *Business Continuity Preparedness Handbook: A Proactive Approach is Key.* Available online at http://www.nascio.org/events/sponsors/vrc/Continuity%20Preparedness%20Handbook,%20August%202011.pdf. Accessed: 23 December 2011.

Avison, D. and Torkzadeh, G. (2009) *Information Systems Project Management.* London: Sage Publications.

Ayadi (2006) Technological and organizational preconditions to Internet banking implementation: case of a Tunisian bank. *Journal of Internet Banking and Commerce,* April 2006, 11(1). Available online at http://www.arraydev.com/commerce/jibc/ Accessed: 12 May 2007.

Baccarini, D. (1999) The logical framework method for defining project success. *Project Management Journal,* December, 25–32.

Banerjee, S. (2007) *Some Challenges in Wireless Security.* Available online at http://moss.csc.ncsu.edu/~mueller/esns07/banerjee.pdf. Accessed: 20 December 2011.

Barbash, A. (2001) Mobile computing for ambulatory health care: points of convergence. *Journal of Ambulatory Care Management,* 244, 54–60.

Beath, C.M., and Orlikowski, W.J. (1994) The contradictory structure of systems development methodologies: deconstructing the IS-user relationship in information engineering. *Information Systems Research,* 5(4), 350–77.

Becher, M. *et al.* (2010) *Mobile Security Catching Up? Revealing the Nuts and Bolts of the Security of Mobile Devices.* Available online at http://www5.rz.rub.de:8032/imperia/md/content/wolf/ieee_mobile.pdf. Accessed: 21 December 2011.

Beer, M. and Nohria, N. (2000) Breaking the code of change. *Harvard Business Review.* May–June. Available at http://webdb.ucs.ed.ac.uk/operations/honsqm/articles/Change2.pdf.

BlackBerry. (2008) *Going Mobile: Developing an Application Mobilization Plan for Your Business.* Available online at http://us.blackberry.com/apps-software/Developing_an_Application_Mobilization_Plan_for_your_Business.pdf. Accessed: 15 January 12.

——(2010) *The CIO's Guide to Mobilizing the Enterprise.* Available online at http://us.blackberry.com/business/leading/2399%20BB%20CIO%20Enterprise%20Guide_V3.pdf. Accessed: 15 January 12.

Branco, P. (2001) Tools and techniques for interaction: challenges for multimodal interfaces towards anyone anywhere accessibility: a position paper, pp. 26–27.

Breu, K., Hemingway, C. and Ashust, C. (2005) The impact of mobile and wireless technology on knowledge workers: an exploratory study, *13th European Conference on Information Systems: Information Systems in a Rapidly Changing Economy*, Paper 79.

Crowley, J. L., Coutaz, J. and Berard, F. (2000) Perceptual user interfaces: things that see. *Communications of the ACM*, 433, 54–64.

Cao, Y. and Cao, R. (1999) Angiogenesis inhibited by drinking tea. *Nature*, 398 (6726): 381.

Cao, Y. Y. and Frank, P. M. (2001). Stability analysis and synthesis of nonlinear time-delay systems via linear Takagi–Sugeno fuzzy models. *Fuzzy sets and systems*, 124(2): 213–29.

Carr, S. (2005) Mobile working: Who wants it? *Silicon.com.* 29–5–2005.

Cerejo, L. (2012) *The Elements of the Mobile User Experience.* http://mobile.smashingmagazine.com/2012/07/12/elements-mobile-user-experience. Accessed 23 November 2012.

Chris, D.C. (2011). Google, NASA and Open Source.

Clarke, S. A. (2007) *Information Systems Strategic Management: An Integrated Approach*, Second Edition. London: Routledge.

Coley Consulting. (2006) *Why Projects Fail.* Retrieved 8 April 2006. Available online at http://www.coleyconsulting.co.uk/failure.htm.

Computer Weekly. (2005) *LondonWaste: A Case Study*, 6 June. Available at www.computerweekly.com/ Accessed 15 December 2011.

Consluim Technologies. (2008) *A Mobile Working Case Study for Swindon Commercial Services (SCS) Part of Swindon Borough.* Available online at Councildownload.microsoft.com/ … /1/9/ … /104_Case_Study_Swindon.pdf. Accessed 25 July 2012.

Cox, T. H. and Blake, S. (1991) Managing cultural diversity: Implications for organizational competitiveness. *The Executive*, 45–56.

Crowley, J.L., Coutaz, J. and Berard, F. (2000) Things that see. *Communications of the Acm* March 43(3): 54–64. Available at http://web.media.mit.edu/~earroyo/thesis-backup/Thesis-prep/ambient%20media/perceptual%20interfaces.pdf.

DeLone, H. and McLean, E. R. (2003) The DeLone and McLean Model of Information Systems Success: A Ten-year Update. *Journal of Management Information Systems*, Spring, 19(4): 9–31.

DeLone, W.H. and McLean, E.R. (1992) Information systems success: the quest for the dependent variable. *Information Systems Research*, 3(1): 60–95.

Doherty, N., Shantanu, B. and Parry, M. (2000). Factors affecting the successful outcome of systems development project. In Beynon-Davies, P., Williams, M.D. and Beeson I. (eds) *Proceedings of the UKAIS Conference on Information Systems, Research. Teaching and Practice*, Cardiff, 26–28 April, pp. 375–83.

Drake, P. and Clarke, S. (2001) *Information Security: A Technical or Human Domain?* IRMA International Conference, Toronto: Human-Side of IT Track.

DTI. (2005) *Achieving best practice in your business: mobile working.* http://www.cobweb.com/pdf/MobileWorkingDTI.pdf

Elliot, D., Swartz, E. and Herbane, B. (1999) Just waiting for the next big bang: business continutity planning in the UK finance sector. *Journal of Applied Management Studies*, 8(1): 43–60.

Endeavour. (2011) *Mobile Weds Cloud – The Perfect Marriage?* Available online at http://your-mobileblog.blogspot.com/2011/11/mobile-weds-cloud-perfect-marriage.html. Accessed 11 January 2012.

——(2011) *The Importance of Mobile Device Management in Enterprise Mobility*. Available online at http://yourmobileblog.blogspot.com/2010/06/importance-of-mobile-device-management.html. Accessed 11 January 2012.

Evans, D. (2004) An introduction to unified communications: challenges and opportunities. *Aslib Proceedings: New Information Perspectives*, pp. 17–20.

Flood, R. L. and Jackson, M. C. (1991) Total Systems Intervention: a practical face to critical systems thinking. In R. L. Flood and M. C. Jackson (eds) *Critical Systems Thinking*. Chichester: John Wiley.

Fonseca, R., Lopez-Garcia, P. and Pissarides, C. A. (2001) Entrepreneurship, start-up costs and employment. *European Economic Review*, 45 (4): 692–705.

Fortune, J. White, D. (2006) Framing of project critical success factors by a systems model. *International Journal of Project Management*, 24(1) January: 53–65.

Gareth, M. (2011) *Mobile Workers Lack Access to Critical Data*. http://www.computing.co.uk/ctg/news/2078877/mobile-workers-lack-access-critical. Accessed 6 January 2012.

Garfinkel, S. (2004) The tablet PC nonrevolution. *Technology Review*, p. 80.

Gauntlett, D. (2007) *Creative Explorations: New Approaches to Identities and Audiences*, London: Routledge.

Gartner (2011) *Gartner Says Apple Will Have a Free Run in Tablet Market Holiday Season as Competitors Continue to Lag*. http://www.gartner.com/newsroom/id/1800514. Accessed 6 January 2012.

Grantham, A. and Tsekouras, G. (2004) Information society: wireless ICTs' transformative potential. *Futures*, 36(3): 359–77.

Greengard, P. *et al.* (2000) Synapsin III: developmental expression, subcellular localization, and role in axon formation. *The Journal of Neuroscience*, 20(10): 3736–44.

Guns, B. (1996) *The Faster Learning Organisation: Gain and Sustain the competitive edge*. San Diego, CA: Pfeiffer – remembering we all need downtime, *Silicon.com*. Accessed 2 December 2004.

Harris, L. and Spence, L. (2002) The ethics of e-banking, *Journal of Electronic Commerce Research*, 3(2): 59–65.

HealthDataManagement. (2005) Exploring barriers to nurse mobile computing. *Health Data Management,* 13(1): 20.

Hoffman, P. (2002) *SMTP service extension for secure SMTP over Transport Layer Security*. Available at http://tools.ietf.org/html/rfc3207.

IDC. (2011a) *Worldwide Mobile Worker Population 2011–15 Forecast*. Doc # 232073 http://www.idc.com/research/viewtoc.jsp?containerId=232073. Accessed 5 April 2013.

——(2011b) *Worldwide Smartphone Market Expected to Grow 55% in 2011 and Approach Shipments of One Billion in 2015*. Available online at http://www.idc.com/getdoc.jsp?containerId=prUS22871611. Accessed 15 January 2012.

——(2011c) *Latest IT News: Cloud Public Market in 2015 Reached a Volume of $72.9 billion*. Available online at http://www.whioam.com/idc-cloud-public-market-in-2015-reached-a-volume-of-729-billion.html. Accessed 11 January 2012.

Ideation. (2011) *Enterprise Mobility Framework*. Available online at http://www.ideationts.com/technology/enterprise-mobility-framework.html. Accessed 11 January 2012.

Jackson, S.E. and Schuler, R.S. (1995) Understanding human resource management in the context of organisations and their environment. In J.T. Spence, J.M. Darley and D.J. Foss (eds) *Annual review of psychology* 46: 237–64. Palo Alto, CA: Annual Reviews, Inc.

Jia S., Lauren B. and Eder, J. (2010) Drew Procaccino: social comparison and trust in the acceptance of social shopping websites. *IJEB*, 8 (4/5): 360–75.

Kakihara, M. and Sorensen, C. (2004) Practising mobile professional work: tales of locational, operational, and interactional mobility. *Info – The journal of policy, regulation and strategy for telecommunications* 63: 180–87.

Kate, P. (2011) *App Adaptation: Enterprise Moving Slowly on Mobile.* http://www.highbeam. com/doc/1G1–254014103.html. Accessed 6 January 2012.

Kellaway, L. (2011) *Scrap Holidays, Bring on the 'Worliday'.* BBC News http://www.bbc.co. uk/news/business-14526949. Accessed 16 August 2011.

Kentrick, C. (2002) The transfer of wireless data: meeting future demand. *Futurics*, 26: 92–107.

Kevin, J. (2010) *Overcoming Security Barriers is Key to Mobile Success.* http://www.paymentssource. com/news/overcoming-security-barriers-key-mobile-success-3003077–1.html. Accessed 6 January 2012.

Knorr, E. Rist, O. (2005). 10 Steps SOA. *InfoWorld*. San Mateo: Nov 7, 2005. 27(45): 23–35. Available online at http://proquest.umi.com/pqdweb?did=930819081&sid=7&Fmt=3&cl ientId=3224&RQT=309&VName=PQD.

Kotter, J. P. (1996) *Leading Change.* Harvard, MA: Harvard Business Press.

Kristen, N. and Trude, D. (2001). *Business Continuity and Disaster Recovery Planning and Management: Perspective* Available online at http://www.availability.com/resource/pdfs/ DPRO-100862.pdf. Accessed 23 December 2011.

Kristoffersen, S. L. F. *Making place to make IT Work: Empirical Explorations of HCI for Mobile CSCW*, pp. 276–85.

Leavitt, Neal. (2011) "Mobile security: Finally a serious problem?" *Computer*. 44(6): 11–14.

Leadent Solutions. (2012) *Case Study – British Gas.* http://www.leadentsolutions.com/Clients/ British-Gas.aspx. Accessed 25 July 2012.

Li, Y.-M. and Yeh, Y.-S. (2010) Increasing Trust in Mobile Commerce through Design Aesthetics, *Computers in Human Behaviour* 26: 673–84. Available at http://www.elsevier. com/locate/comphumbeh. Accessed 10 April 2011.

Lipovertsky, S., Tishler, A., Dvir, D. and Shenhar, A. (1997) The relative importance of project success dimensions. *R 106.*

Lookout Mobile Security. (2011) *2011 Mobile Threat Report.* Available online at https:// www.mylookout.com/mobile-threat-report. Accessed 18 December 2011.

——(2011) *2011 Mobile Threat Report Finds Users Are 2.5X as Likely to Encounter Malware.* Available online at http://blog.mylookout.com/blog/2011/08/02/2011-mobile-threat-report- finds-users-are-2-5x-as-likely-to-encounter-malware/. Accessed 18 December 2011.

Lyytinen, K. (1987) Information systems failure: a survey and classification of the empirical literature. In Zorkoczy, P. I. (ed.) *Oxford Surveys in Information Technology*, 4 Oxford: Oxford University Press, pp. 257–309.

McAfee. (2008). *McAfee Mobile Security Report 2008.* Available online at http://www.mcafee. com/us/resources/reports/rp-mobile-security-2008.pdf. Accessed 19 December 2011.

——(2011) *McAfee Threats Report: Third Quarter 2011.* Available online at http://www.mca fee.com/us/resources/reports/rp-quarterly-threat-q3–2011.pdf. Accessed 19 December 2011.

McCue, A. (2005) Remote workers feel alienated and mistrusted. *Silicon.com.* Accessed 29 May 2005.

McDougall, P. (2007) Credit Suisse outsources to BT in deal worth $1.1 billion. *Information Week.* February 13.

Milanesi, C. (2011) iPad and beyond: the future of the tablet market. 2 September. Available at http://www.gartner.com/id=1782214. Accessed 5 January 2012.

Minder, C. (2004) A methodology for building mobile computing applications. *International Journal of Electronic Business*, 2(3): 229.

Mintzberg, H. (1998) Politics and the political organisation. In Mintzberg, H., Quinn J. B. and Ghoshal, S. (eds) *The Strategy Process*, Revised European Edition, London: Prentice Hall, pp. 377–82.

Motorola. (2008) *2G and 3G Cellular Networks: Their Impact on Today's Enterprise Mobility Solutions and Future.* Available online at http://www.bm-tricon.com/images/doku/ motorola_2g-and-3g-cellular-networks.pdf. Accessed 10 January 2012.

Murray, A. (2008) Best practice focus-PRINCE2 will get an overhaul for 2009. Andy Murray will be disclosing some of the developments at the BPUG congress in February. BPUG Congress news. *Project Manager Today*, p 25.

Nortel. (2008) *Mobile Unified Communications: Extending Enterprise Communications to Mobile Phones for Lower Costs and a Simplified User Experience.* http://www.acctel.ca/docs/Mobile%20Unified%20Communications.pdf. Accessed 6 January 2012.

Overland Storage. (2010) *A Practical Guide to Business Continuity.* Available online at http://www.overlandstorage.com/pdfs/PracticalGuide2BC_whitepaper_0213.pdf. Accessed 23 December 2011.

Panda Security. (2011) *More than 5 Million New Malware Samples in the Last Quarter of Year.* Available online at http://press.pandasecurity.com/news/more-than-5-million-new-malware-samples-in-the-last-quarter-of-the-year-report-pandalabs/. Accessed 19 December 2011.

Pascoe, J. R. N. M. D. (2002) Using while moving: HCI issues in fieldwork environments. *ACM Transactions on Computer-Human Interaction (TOCHI)* 7(3): 417–37.

Perry, M., O'Hara, K., Sellen, A., Brown, B. and Harper, R. (2001) Dealing with Mobility: Understanding Access Anytime, Anywhere. *ACM Transactions on Computer-Human Interaction* 8(4): 323–47.

Peter, L. *et al.* (2011) *Connected Agriculture: The Role of Mobile in Driving Efficiency and Sustainability in the Food and Agriculture Value Chain.* http://www.vodafone.com/content/dam/vodafone/about/sustainability/2011/pdf/connected_agriculture.pdf. Accessed 3 January 2012.

Peters, O. and Allouch, S. V. (2005) Always connected: a longitudinal field study of mobile communication. *Telematics and Informatics*, 22(3): 239–56.

Pettigrew, A. M. (1985) Contextualist research: a natural way to link theory and practice. *Doing Research that is Useful in Theory and Practice*, pp. 222–73.

Phifer, L. (2004) "Roaming Far And Wide With Mobile VPNs", *Business Communications Review*, 34(9): 42–47.

Porn, L. M. and Patrick, K. (2002) Mobile computing acceptance grows as applications evolve, *Healthcare Financial Management*, 56(1): 66–70.

Procaccino, J.D. and Verner, J. M. (2006) Software project managers and project success: An exploratory study. *The Journal of Systems and Software*, 79:1541–51

Pugh, E. D. L., Hinton, E., and Zienkiewicz, O. C. (1978). A study of quadrilateral plate bending elements with 'reduced'integration. *International Journal for Numerical Methods in Engineering*, 12 (7): 1059–79.

Rehman, S.U. and Coughlan. J.-L. (2011) *Building Trust of Mobile Users and Their Adoption of M-Commerce, World Academy of Science, Engineering and Technology* 75: 593–95. Available at http://www.waset.org/journals/waset/v75/v75–105.pdf Accessed 29 April 2011.

Revathy, L. N. (2004) "'Designed' to follow", *Businessline*, p. 1.

Riederer, M. A., Soldati, T., Shapiro, A. D., Lin, J. and Pfeffer, S. R. (1994) Lysosome biogenesis requires Rab9 function and receptor recycling from endosomes to the trans-Golgi network. *The Journal of cell biology*, 125(3): 573–82.

Rules, O. (2012). *Operations Strategy Implications for the 'Decline of the PC' Era.* Available online at http://www.business2community.com/tech-gadgets/operations-strategy-implications-for-the-decline-of-the-pc-era-0271580. Accessed 25 December 12.

Sandra, P. and Nathan, D. (2008) *Maximizing Mobile Worker Productivity.* http://www.himss.org/content/files/MaximizingMobileProductivity.pdf. Accessed: 6th Jan 2012.

SAP. (2005) *IBM Lotus Integration with SAP Enterprise Portal – An Overview.* Available online at http://www.sdn.sap.com/irj/scn/index?rid=/library/uuid/9727ea90–0201-0010-be8e-b649280fe6ff. Accessed 10 January 2012.

Sarah, P. (2009) *Are Mobile Botnets in Our Future?* Available online at http://www.readwriteweb.com/archives/are_mobile_botnets_in_our_future.php. Accessed 18 December 2011.

Schrott, G. and Gluckler, J. (2004) What makes mobile computer supported cooperative work mobile? Towards a better understanding of cooperative mobile interactions, *International Journal of Human-Computer Studies*, 60(5–6): 737–52.

SearchDomino. (2004) *Lotus Workplace.* Available online at http://searchdomino.techtarget.com/definition/Lotus-Workplace. Accessed 10 January 2012.

Seddon, P. B., (1997) A respecification and extension of the DeLone and McLean model of IS success. *Information Systems Research*, 8(3): 240–53.

Shenhar, A.J., Dvir, D., Levy, O. and Maltz, A. (2001) Project success: a multidimensional strategic concept. *Long Range Planning*, 34: 699–725.

Shenhar, A. J., Tishler, A., Dvir, D., Lipovetsky, S. and Lechler, T. (2002) Refining the search for project success factors: a multivariate, typological approach. *Research 26.*

Silicon, S. (2005) Flexible working will wipe out middle managers. *www.silicon.com.*

Sohr, K., Mustafa, T. and Nowak, A. (2011) *Software Security Aspects of Java-Based Mobile Phones. Symposium on Applied Computing,* Available at: http://www.informatik.uni-bremen.de/~sohr/papers/sac11.pdf Accessed 02 May 2011.

Spriestersbach, A., Vogler, H., Lehmann F. and Ziegert, T. (2001) Integrating context information into enterprise applications for the mobile workforce – A case study. *WMC '01 Proceedings of the 1st International Workshop on Mobile Commerce,* pp. 55–59.

Stedman, L. (2004) Flexible Friends. *Utility Week* 22(9): 26–27.

Storkey, I. (2011) *Operational Risk Management and Business Continuity Planning for Modern State Treasuries.* Available online at http://www.imf.org/external/pubs/ft/tnm/2011/tnm1105.pdf. Accessed 23 December 2011.

Suitor, J. J., Wellman, B. and David, L. M. (1997) It's about time: how, why, and when networks change. *Social Networks,* 19(1): 1–7.

Sybase. (2010) *Sybase Unwired Platform: Mobile Enterprise Application Platform.* Available online at http://www.virtualtechtour.com/assets/mobility/SUP_Solution_Brief.pdf. Accessed 15 January 2012.

——(2011) *Enterprise Mobility Guild 2011.* Available online at http://www.sap.com/denmark/solutions/mobility/pdf/Enterprise_Mobility_Guide_2011.pdf. Accessed 15 January 2012.

Teo, T. S., and Too, B. L. (2000) Information systems orientation and business use of the Internet: An empirical study. *International Journal of Electronic Commerce,* 105–30.

Truste. (2011) *Mobile Privacy Survey Results.* http://www.truste.com/why_TRUSTe_privacy_services/harris-mobile-survey. Accessed 23 November 2012.

U.S. Department of Homeland Security. *Federal Information Security Management Act (FISMA), Sec. 3542.* Available online at http://www.marcorsyscom.usmc.mil/sites/pmia%20documents/documents/Federal%20Information%20Security%20Management%20Act%20(FISMA).htm. Accessed 20 December 2011.

Varshney, U. (2000) Recent advances in wired networking. *Computer,* 33(4): 107–9.

Wang, Y. D. and Emurian, H. H. (2005). An overview of online trust: concepts, elements, and implications. *Computers in Human Behaviour,* 21: 105–25.

Wirelessnews. (2004) Siemens study: workers say fragmented communication tools and devices produce fewer answers. *Wireless News,* 1.

Webster's Online Dictionary. (2006) *Definition: Groupware.* Available online at http://www.websters-online-dictionary.org/definitions/groupware. Accessed 10 January 12.

York, J. and Pendharkar, P. C. (2004) Human-computer interaction issues for mobile computing in a variable work context, *International Journal of Human-Computer Studies,* 60 (5–6): 771–97.

Young, R. D., Lang, W. W. and Nolle, D. L. (2007) How the Internet affects output and performance at community banks. *Journal of Banking 60.*

Zahra, S. A. and George, G. (2002) Absorptive capacity: A review, reconceptualization, and extension. *Academy of Management Review,* pp. 185–203.

Zeus, K. (2008) *Accelerating Unified Communications with an Enterprise-Wide Architecture.* http://www.e-telsystems.com/documents/Accelerating_Unified_Communications.pdf. Accessed 7 January 2012.

Further reading

3gpp. (2006) *LTE Advanced.* Available at http://www.3gpp.org/LTE-Advanced. Accessed 2 May 2011.

4G Mobile Phone Network Comes to Scandinavia. Online 14 December 2009. Available at http://news.bbc.co.uk/1/hi/technology/8412035.stm. Accessed 15 April 2011.

ABIresearch. (2010) *Shopping by Mobile Will Grow to $119 Billion in 2015*. Available at http://www.abiresearch.com/press/1605-Shopping+by+Mobile+Will+Grow+to+$119+Billion+in+2015. Accessed 13 April 2011

Becker, S. A. (2005). Technical opinion: e-government usability for older adults. *Communications of the ACM*, 48(2): 102–4.

Berger, S.C. Gensler, S. (2007) Online Banking Customers: Insights from Germany. *Journal of Internet Banking and Commerce*, 12(1) April.

Bhalla, M. R. and A. V. Bhalla (2010) Generations of mobile wireless technology: a survey, *International Journal of Computer Applications* (0975 – 8887) 5(4): 26–32. Available at http://www.ijcaonline.org/volume5/number4/pxc3871282.pdf Accessed 18 April 2011.

Butcher, D. (2011) *Amazon eyes NFC as next front in mobile commerce format war*. Available at http://www.mobilecommercedaily.com/2011/04/05/amazon-eyes-nfc-as-next-front-in-mobile-commerce-format-war. Accessed 13 April.

Charlton, G. (2010) *Are UK Retailers Interested in Mobile Commerce?* Available at http://econsultancy.com/uk/blog/5734-are-uk-retailers-interested-in-mobile-commerce. Accessed 15 April 2011.

Choi, D.-Y. (2007) Personalized local internet in the location-based mobile web search, *Decision Support Systems*, 43 (1): 31–45. Available at http://www.informatik.uni-trier.de/~ley/db/journals/dss/dss43.html#choi07. Accessed 10 April 2011.

Consilium Technologies (2008) Swindon commercial case study. Available at http://www.totalmobile.co.uk/resources/viewer/index/case_studies/swindon-commercial-case-study. Accessed 10 April 2011.

Dejean, D. (2007) *Good Riddance TO IBM Workplace*. Available online at http://www.informationweek.com/blog/main/archives/2007/01/good_riddance_t.html. Accessed 10 January 2012.

Dubelaar, C., Sohal, A. and Savic, V. (2005) Benefits, impediments and critical success factors in B2C. E-business adoption. *Technovation*, 25: 1251–62.

Eric, B. (2011) *Android Malware on the Rise, but Google Says the Threat's Overblown*. Available online at http://www.linuxfordevices.com/c/a/News/McAfee-3Q-2011-malware-report/. Accessed 19 December 2011.

Hibberd, J. (2010) 18–34 *Year Olds Drive European Adoption of Mobile Commerce*. Available at http://mmaglobal.com/news/18–34-year-olds-drive-european-adoption-mobile-commerce. Accessed 8 April 2011.

Ho, S.-Y., Chen, J.-C. and Chen, C.-C. (2010) Deconstruct Technology Products Design – Take the Smart Phone as Examples, *New Trends in Information Science and Service Science (NISS), 2010 4th International Conference*. Online pp. 569–73. Available at http://ieeexplore.ieee.org/Xplore/login.jsp?url=http%3A%2F%2Fieeexplore.ieee.org%2Fiel5%2F5480449%2F5488502%2F05488551.pdf%3Farnumber%3D5488551&authDecision=-203. Accessed 15 April 2011.

Ip, B. (2008) Technological, content, and market convergence in the games industry, rpt. *Games and Culture*, 23(2) April: 199–224. Available at http://ieeexplore.ieee.org:80/xpl/ Accessed 10 April 2011.

Jhones, K. (2011) *M – Commerce the new way of Communication in the Future Business*. Available at http://theguidetohomebusinesssuccess.com/theguide/m-commerce-the-new-way-of-communication-in-the-future-business/. Accessed 20 April 2011.

Khan, M.A. (2010) The Danger that Amazon's $1B in Mobile Commerce Poses for Other Retailers, July 26, 2010, *Mobile Commerce Daily* Available at http://www.mobilecommercedaily.com/2010/07/26/the-danger-that-amazon's-1b-in-mobile-commerce-poses-for-other-retailers Accessed 3 April 2011.

Kim, C., Mirusmonov, M. and Lee, I. (2010) An empirical examination of factors influencing the intention to use mobile payment, *Computers in Human Behaviour* 26 (2010) pp. 310–322. Available at http://portal.acm.org/citation.cfm?id=1750030&preflayout=flat#prox Accessed 19 April 2011.

Kraemer, K. and Dedrick, J. (2001) *Dell Computer: Using E-commerce To Support the Virtual Company*. Available at http://crito.uci.edu/papers/2001/dell_ecom_case_6–13-01.pdf. Accessed 7th April 2010.

Leavitt, N. (2010) Payment applications make e-commerce mobile, *Technology News* rpt in *Computer* 43(12) December: 19–22. Available at http://ieeexplore.ieee.org Accessed 10 April 2011.

Leavitt, N. (2011) *Mobile Security: Finally a Serious Problem?* Available online at http://www.leavcom.com/pdf/Mobilesecurity.pdf. Accessed: 21 December 2011.

Luo, X., Li, H., Zhang, J. and Shim, J.-P. (2010) Examining multi-dimensional trust and multi-faceted risk in initial acceptance of emerging technologies: An empirical study of mobile banking services. *Decision Support Systems*, 49:222–34. Available at http://www.sciencedirect.com/science?_ob=ArticleURLudi=B6V8S-4YG7JPJuser=122875coverDate=05%2F31%2F2010rdoc=1fmt=highorig=gatewayorigin=gatewaysort=ddocanchor=&view=csearchStrId=1736759862rerunOrigin=scholar.googleacct= C000010098version=1url Version=0userid=122875&md5=89f1fd696a047f5671be24ff4a1a48f9&searchtype=a Accessed 10 April 2011.

Mahatanankoon, P. and Vila-Ruiz, J. (2008) Why won't consumers adopt m-commerce? : an exploratory study, *Journal of Internet Commerce*, 6(4): 113–28. Available at http://www.informaworld.com/smpp/content~content=a904333273~db=all~jumptype=rss Accessed 19 March 2011.

Miller, P. (2010) Visa rolling out paywave mobile phone payments in NY subway and taxis. *Blog* posted 23 September 2010. Available at http://www.engadget.com/2010/09/23/visa-rolling-out-paywave-mobile-phone-payments-in-ny-subway-and/ Accessed 17 April 2011.

MOBIFY. (2011) *Tablets, Mobile E-Commerce and Mobify*. Available at http://blog.mobify.me/2011/03/09/tablets-mobile-e-commerce-and-mobify/. Accessed 20 April 2011.

Mobile Squared. (2011) *Tesco Outlines Connected Strategy for all Retailers to Follow*. Available at http://www.mobilesquared.co.uk/news/3285. Accessed 16 April 11.

Murphy, D. (2011) *The Decline of the Dongle*. Available at http://www.mobilemarketingmagazine.com/content/decline-dongle. Accessed 16 April 2011.

Ngai, E.W.T. (2007) *Learning in introductory e-commerce: A project-based teamwork approach*. Available at http://www.sciencedirect.com

Nguyen, A. (2011) Ladbrokes to expand investment in mobile for growth. Available at http://www.computerworlduk.com/news/mobile-wireless/3261573/ladbrokes-to-expand-investment-in-mobile-for-growth/. Accessed 11 April 2011.

O'Sullivan, C. (2010) Mobile Networks finally find out what 4G means, *GoMo News* 24 November. Available at http://www.gomonews.com/mobile-networks-finally-find-out-what-4g-means/ Accessed 17 April 2011.

Oxford Dictionaries. (2011). *m-commerce*. Available athttp://oxforddictionaries.com/view/entry/m_en_gb0506850#m_en_gb0506850. Accessed 7 December 2010.

Pirakatheeswari, P. (2009) *Introduction To Electronic Retailing*. Available at http://www.articlesbase.com/online-business-articles/introduction-to-electronic-retailing-1058777.html. Accessed 7 April 2010.

PRWeb. (2011) Smartphone adoption and App Stores push European mobile betting user base past 2 million, *Juniper Report finds*, Available at http://uk.prweb.com/releases/2010/10/prweb4612274.htm. Accessed 20 April 2011.

Raja, S. (2004) One window will do. *Businessline*, 1.

Ranger, S. (2005) Flexible working will wipe out middle managers. May 24. *Silicon*.

Ratten, V. (2010) E-book devices and m-commerce: what might be the impact on organisational learning? *Development and Learning in Organisations: An International Journal*, 24(6): 6–7. Available at http://search.informit.com.au/documentSummary;dn=448757461396509 Accessed 17 April 2011.

Shah, M. H. and Siddiqui, F. A. (2006) Organisational success factors in e-banking at the Woolwich. *International Journal of Information Management*, 26: 442–56.

Shah, M. H., Braganza, A. and Morabito, V. (2007) A survey of critical success factors in e-banking: an organisational perspective *European Journal of Information Systems*, 16(4): 511–24. http://www.palgrave-journals.com/ejis/journal/v16/n4/index.html.

Shah, M.H. and Clarke, S. (2009) E-banking management: issues, solutions and strategies. *IGI Global*, US.

Shankar, U. and Sultan, F. (2002) Online trust: a stakeholder perspective, concepts, implications and future directions. *Journal of Strategic Information Systems*, pp. 325–44.

Shields, R. and Charara, S. (2011) *Fashion Retailers Lead Charge into Mobile Shopping*. Available at http://www.nma.co.uk/news/cover-story-fashion-etailers-lead-charge-into-mobile-shopping/3022697.article. Accessed 18 April 2011.

Siau, K. and Shen, Z. (2003) Building Customer Trust in Mobile Commerce, *Communications of the ACN*, 46(4) April: 91–94. Available at http://delivery.acm.org/10.1145/650000/641211p91-siau.pdf?key1=641211&key2=1794524031&coll=DL&dl=ACM&ip=193.61.255.87&CFID=20546659&CFTOKEN=15228874 Accessed 25 April 2011.

Skeldon, P. (2011) Businesses have to avoid making same mistakes with mobile as they did with the nascent web, warns roundtable. Available at http://www.internetretailing.net/2011/03/businesses-have-to-avoid-making-same-mistakes-with-mobile-as-they-did-with-the-nascent-web-warns-roundtable/. Accessed 14 April 2011.

Slivka, E. (2011) *Ipad Set for 'Free Run' Through Holiday Tablet Shopping Season*. Available online at http://www.macrumors.com/2011/09/22/ipad-set-for-free-run-through-holiday-tablet-shopping-season. Accessed 25 December 2012.

Stahl, B.C. (2008) *Information Systems Critical Perspectives*. London: Routledge.

Stephen, D., Jaffe, J. and Raymond, B. (2010) *Worldwide Mobile Worker Population 2009–2012 Forecast*. Available at http://www.gotomypc.com/remote_access/images/pdf/How_to_Equip_Your_Company_for_the_New_Mobile_Workforce.pdf. Accessed 3 January 2012.

Syputa, R. (2009) *What is the Difference Between WIMax and LTE*. Available at http://www.telecomcircle.com/2009/09/what-is-the-difference-between-wimax-and-lte/. Accessed 11 April 2011

ThaiVisa. (2011) *South Korea Develops World's First 4G Mobile System*. Available at http://www.thaivisa.com/forum/topic/137166-south-korea-develops-worlds-first-4g-mobile-system/. Accessed 06 April 2011.

Turbin, E., Lee, J. King D. and Chung, H. M. (2002). *Electronic Commerce: A Managerial Perspective*. International edition. Prentice Hall, London.

Weißenberg, N., Voisard, A. and Gartmann, R. (2004) *Using Ontologies in Personalized Mobile Applications*. Available at: http://compass.dfki.de/Internal/Deliverables/userRequirements/references/ACM-GIS04-p029-weissenberg2.pdf

Xu, L.D. (2007) *Frontiers in Enterprise Integration*. London: Routledge.

INDEX

Printed in the United States
by Baker & Taylor Publisher Services